Microsoft SQL Server 2008 High Availability

Minimize downtime, speed up recovery, and achieve
the highest level of availability and reliability for
SQL server applications by mastering the concepts
of database mirroring, log shipping, clustering,
and replication

Hemantgiri S. Goswami

BIRMINGHAM - MUMBAI

Microsoft SQL Server 2008 High Availability

First published: January 2011

Production Reference: 2170111

Published by Packt Publishing Ltd.
32 Lincoln Road
Olton
Birmingham, B27 6PA, UK.

ISBN 978-1-849681-22-3

www.packtpub.com

Cover Image by Mark Holland (mJH767@bham.ac.uk)

Credits

Author
Hemantgiri S. Goswami

Reviewers
Adam Haines

Deepak Vohra

Development Editor
Maitreya Bhakal

Technical Editor
Gaurav Datar

Copy Editors
Leonard D'Silva

Janki Mathuria

Indexer
Monica Ajmera Mehta

Editorial Team Leader
Gagandeep Singh

Project Team Leader
Ashwin Shetty

Project Coordinator
Joel Goveya

Proofreader
Mario Cecere

Graphics
Geetanjali Sawant

Production Coordinator
Shantanu Zagade

Cover Work
Shantanu Zagade

Foreword

Every new version of SQL Server brings with it new tools and features for database administrators (DBAs), developers, and architects, for them to be able to provide an effective solution for the end users in a simpler and more efficient manner. The terms effective and efficiency can be measured in a technical perspective as High Availability (HA) and Disaster Recovery (DR).

Let's assume that a world-wide retailer's CTO has been tasked to provide high availability for their mission-critical back-end systems that are built upon SQL Server technologies. It is a major task for DBAs to implement an HA solution on a SQL Server data platform, and for developers to ensure that underlying application architecture is HA-aware to take advantage of mission-critical features from SQL Server technologies.

SQL Server High Availability features include failover clustering, database mirroring, log shipping, replication, and backup and restore strategies. The solution must fit within the company's budget, keeping up the scalability, and should reduce degradation in performance. When it comes to the disaster recovery solution, it may not be possible for the primary and secondary site's hardware to be the same, such as fewer hardware resources, limited storage capacity, or data center limitations. It may be acceptable to the business in terms of costing, but when a disaster strikes, the damage will be irrecoverable. All such out-of-the-box limitations must be avoided, or reduced, to keep up the mission-critical applications always online.

The most critical aspect of any high-availability solution is designing a failback (quick recovery of data) strategy, that is, the application must be designed to direct the connections to the available instance when the SQL Server instance fails over to the secondary server in a seamless manner. Though SQL Server is an out-of-the-box disaster recovery tool, many of them are limited to traditional methods of backup and restore functionality that are time consuming during a recovery event. So, the new trend in the industry is to replace the existing older backup and restore policies, taking advantage of hardware capabilities as a DR solution. This requires server-class hardware and standardization on same hardware, but still lacks the quicker data recovery strategy.

To overcome the point-in-time data recovery problems, an enterprise-level HA solution is essential. This is where SQL Server provides such a business value proposition for the end users.

To be a competent DBA, developer, or architect, a firm grasp of tools and features is highly essential. The internal architecture of SQL Server provides a great deal on HA and DR capabilities. Similarly, this book can be helpful as a roadmap when working on your own to succeed in implementing high availability features and technology, with the help of SQL Server 2008 version.

A giant leap starts with a small step. Similarly, to begin with HA and DR solution implementation, the underlying architecture of SQL Server 2008 (and higher) will provide a good foundation to your existing data platform. This book covers the key aspects of important features of SQL Server high availability, along with a tour on best practices implementation. The book starts with a clear explanation, to enable the readers to understand how the SQL Server security mechanism works and how tightly it is integrated in the Windows domain.

It covers the itemized measures to take on the out-of-SQL Server environment such as understanding the importance of windows domains, domain users, and the security measures to benefit from the latest version of SQL Server. Then it cruises through the implementation of clusters with a best example scenario that will help users set up a multi-instance SQL Server failover cluster with a specific difference between single-instance and multi-instance SQL Server failover cluster nodes. The first chapter touches on Windows Hyper-V technology, specific component configuration in a failover cluster environment, and advantages of the multi-instance failover cluster over the single-instance failover cluster. This is a best illustration on how a road map should begin and helps design a high-availability solution.

So, when it comes to mission-critical support for your SQL Server data platform, the pool of SQL Server technologies resources is out there. But keep in mind that the advantage of SQL Server can be implemented in various configurations for different purposes, and so finding a single resource with everything you need may prove difficult. In any case or scenario, this book will help users through the comprehensive levels of HA and DR implementation for their data platform needs.

Satya Shyam K Jayanty (SQL Server MVP)
Principal Architect & Director D Bi A Solutions Limited

About the Author

Hemantgiri S. Goswami is an SQL Server MVP, working as a Database Architect in NetDScure Services, Surat, India. He has been a Microsoft SQL Server MVP for three years. He moderates multiple SQL Server community forums, including `http://www.sql-server-performance.com` and `http://www.sqlserver-qa.net`. He actively participates in and speaks at local user group events, organized under the aegis of `http://www.surat-user-group.org`, the Surat chapter of DotNetChaps and CSI, of which he is a founding and active member. He regularly publishes articles on his blog space at `http://www.sql-server-citation.com`. He has recently taken up a new initiative—blogging about SQL in his mother tongue Gujarati, through his blog at `http://sqlservercitation-gujarati.blogspot.com`.

He has more than 11 years of experience in the IT industry, for nine years of which he was working as a hardcore DBA focusing on High Availability area. During his stint of 11 years in the IT field, he has worked with the top five IT giants of India. In addition to SQL Server, Hemantgiri also possesses excellent knowledge of Windows Server OS(s) and Networking.

In his free time, he prefers watching cartoons, reading, and even sketching at times.

You can reach him via his blog, on Twitter, or by writing to him at `hemantgiri@sql-server-citation.com`.

Acknowledgement

This is the first book I have written and I would like to dedicate this book to my better half, my wife Rachana, and to my parents. Without their support and encouragement, I couldn't have completed this book at all. Writing a book requires a great amount of time, which kept me away from my family completely, especially on weekends. Rachana shouldered almost all responsibility of the family while I was busy writing this book, so a very special thanks to her.

I would also like to acknowledge the contribution of Sunny Kansara, who introduced me to Packt Publishing as a writer. Prior to this, I was only writing for my own blog space and some of the SQL Server community websites and had never given a thought to writing such a book until Sunny came along. I sincerely appreciate the efforts of Rashmi Phadnis in giving this book a proper flow and character by correcting my writing. Without her, my writing would not have been as meaningful for readers as it is now; thank you Rashmi. I will like to thank the Technical Editor for this book, Gaurav, as well the Development Editor, Maitreya, for their sincere efforts. Last but definitely not the least, I would like to thank the Project Coordinator, Joel, for his unflinching support and the patience he has shown with my erratic writing schedules. My thanks to Deepak Vohra, Adam Haines, and Parag Paithankar, who contributed their efforts to review this book technically with a keen observation.

It took me over five months to complete this first book. When I would return home after a full-day at the office and would be about to start writing, Dhruti, my bundle of joy (my 18 months-old daughter) would also want to see her cartoon movies on my laptop at the same time. To distract her, I would invariably have to put on her favorite rhymes, and after listening to two or three rhymes, she would allow me to get back to my writing work. It made for a happy distraction; I love you a lot my darling.

I have attempted to put on paper, with the help of this book, all the knowledge I have acquired about SQL Server. While I have done my best, I know that in many areas, I might not be perfect. As this is my first book, I also know that I have taken many undue liberties with writing. I hope my readers will forgive me and overlook this fact. I am still learning.

I hope you enjoy reading and learning from this book, as it would give me a lot of satisfaction that in some small way, I have contributed to the growth and propagation of knowledge about my beloved SQL Server.

About the Reviewers

Adam Haines is a Microsoft Certified Professional Database Administrator and Developer, based in New Orleans, Louisiana. Adam has been working with database technology since 2004. Adam started his career in the banking industry, where he assumed the position of Database Analyst. While in this role, he focused on database development, report writing, application programming, and database administration. In 2007, he accepted a Database Administrator position at Stewart Enterprises Inc. His current position requires him to focus on database development; however, Adam still manages administrative duties. He has experience in database administration, performance tuning and optimization, SQL Server High Availability, SSIS, Analysis Services, SSRS, Data Warehousing, Disaster Recovery, and Web/ Windows development. When Adam has downtime, he volunteers his time to the SQL Server community by moderating and answering questions on the MSDN SQL Server forums. He is also part of the team at TSQLChallenges.com. In his role at TSQLChallenges.com, Adam creates, evaluates, and moderates SQL Server puzzles. He has been recognized by Microsoft for his knowledge and contributions to the SQL Server community, by being awarded the SQL Server Most Valuable Professional (MVP) status.

First, I would like to thank Kent Waldrop, a fellow SQL Server MVP. Kent is a great friend and mentor. Kent kept me motivated and helped cultivate my passion for SQL Server. Had it not been for Kent's mentorship, I may not be where I am today.

I would also like to thank my family, which is the cornerstone of my life. They have been very understanding and supportive of my time dedicated to extracurricular SQL Server commitments. Without the support and love of my family, I would not have had the great life I enjoy today.

Deepak Vohra is a consultant and a principal member of NuBean.com, a software company. Deepak is a Sun Certified Java Programmer and Web Component Developer, and has worked in the fields of XML, Java programming, and J2EE for over five years. Deepak is the co-author of *Pro XML Development with Java Technology*, a book by Apress, and was the technical reviewer for *WebLogic: The Definitive Guide*, an O'Reily book. Deepak was also the technical reviewer for the Course Technology PTR book *Ruby Programming for the Absolute Beginner*, and the technical editor for *Prototype and Scriptaculous in Action*, by Manning Publications. Deepak has also written the following two books for Packt Publishing: *JDBC 4.0 and Oracle JDeveloper for J2EE Development* and *Processing XML Documents with Oracle JDeveloper 11g*.

www.PacktPub.com

Support files, eBooks, discount offers and more

You might want to visit www.PacktPub.com for support files and downloads related to your book.

Did you know that Packt offers eBook versions of every book published, with PDF and ePub files available? You can upgrade to the eBook version at www.PacktPub.com and as a print book customer, you are entitled to a discount on the eBook copy. Get in touch with us at service@packtpub.com for more details.

At www.PacktPub.com, you can also read a collection of free technical articles, sign up for a range of free newsletters and receive exclusive discounts and offers on Packt books and eBooks.

http://PacktLib.PacktPub.com

Do you need instant solutions to your IT questions? PacktLib is Packt's online digital book library. Here, you can access, read and search across Packt's entire library of books.

Why Subscribe?

- Fully searchable across every book published by Packt
- Copy and paste, print and bookmark content
- On demand and accessible via web browser

Free Access for Packt account holders

If you have an account with Packt at www.PacktPub.com, you can use this to access PacktLib today and view nine entirely free books. Simply use your login credentials for immediate access.

Table of Contents

Preface

The term **High Availability** means that the servers or systems that host or run the business-critical applications should be highly available 24 X 7. As the word itself defines how important it is to make these applications and data available for end-users as well as business users, if this data is not available for a short time, it will be a big problem for both sets of users. Imagine a bank spread across the country and having a huge customer base. One fine day, their server crashes! If the bank relies only on backups, then it might end up losing approximately 15 to 30 minutes of data, depending on the backup strategy. However, the HA options related to SQL Server such as clustering, replication, log shipping, and database mirroring will help overcome this situation.

By the end of the book, you will be able to find yourself in a position where you can easily install and configure the different High Available solutions for SQL Server. You will also be able to troubleshoot most common issues yourself by following the troubleshooting appendix.

What this book covers

Chapter 1, Understanding Windows Domains, Domain Users, and SQL Server Security, will help you understand what is Windows domain, what are domain users, and the basic security concepts for Windows and SQL Server to get yourself prepared for the next chapter.

Chapter 2, Implementing Clustering, will help you understand the prerequisites for SQL Server Clustering and guide you on how to install and configure SQL Server Cluster using both T-SQL and SSMS. The chapter also helps you on how to add or remove a node from an existing cluster.

Chapter 3, Snapshot Replication, will help you understand prerequisites for installing Snapshot Replication using SQL Server. It guides you in installing and configuring Snapshot Replication using both T-SQL and SSMS.

Chapter 4, Transactional Replication, will give you information on how to install and configure Transactional Replication. It also helps you understand how replication works and the different options available to configure and install Transactional Replication.

Chapter 5, Merge Replication, helps you install and configure Merge Replication. It also makes you understand the different components of Merge Replication, and how it works. It guides you on how to configure Merge Replication, using both T-SQL and SSMS.

Chapter 6, Peer-to-Peer Replication, explains how to install and configure Peer-to-Peer Replication, using both T-SQL and GUI. It also explains how to add or remove nodes.

Chapter 7, Log Shipping, describes what Log Shipping is, how it works, and what are the prerequisite components for its installation. The chapter also helps understand how to install Log Shipping using both T-SQL and SSMS.

Chapter 8, Database Mirroring, explains what Database Mirroring is all about, how it works, and what are the different components we need to implement it. We also learn different types of Database Mirroring and how to install and configure it using both T-SQL and SSMS.

Appendix A, Troubleshooting, contains the troubleshooting tips for the common issues faced in all of the previous chapters.

Appendix B, External References, contains the external references that we might need to refer, in order to gain further information on topics covered in all of the previous eight chapters.

What you need for this book

High Availability options can be used to make systems or servers highly available, so that the work isn't hindered in case of any emergency or failure of resources. So, to make your system and server capable of installing SQL Server 2008 High availability options such as clustering, replication, database mirroring, and log shipping, the following are the prerequisites:

* Processor type: Pentium-3 or higher.
* Processor speed: 1.0 Gigahertz or higher.
* RAM: At least 512 MB, but 2 GB is recommended.
* Display: VGA or higher resolution.

- Operating system: Windows 7 Ultimate, Windows Server 2003 (x86 or x64) , Windows Server 2008 (x86 or x64).

- Disk space: Minimum 1 GB.

- .NET framework.

- Windows Installer 4.5 or later.

- Microsoft Data Access Component (MDAC) 2.8 SP1 or later. MDAC can be obtained from `http://go.microsoft.com/fwlink/?LinkId=50233`.

For complete information on prerequisites, a reader can refer to the prerequisites section of each chapter.

You may refer to the external references for the further reading and can post back your queries to any SQL Server forums out their such as `http://www.sql-server-performance.com` or `www.surat-user-group.org/forums`.

Who this book is for

If you are a SQL Server Developer, or a System Administrator, or even a novice DBA, then this book is for you. It requires you to have only a basic understanding of how SQL Server works to get you through the installation of SQL Server HA.

Conventions

In this book, you will find a number of styles of text that distinguish between different kinds of information. Here are some examples of these styles, and an explanation of their meaning.

Code words in text are shown as follows: "We should set the value as `true` for the `@stream_blob_columns` of `sp_addmergearticle` parameter if there are LOB data types to publish."

A block of code is set as follows:

```
use [ReportServer$SQL2008R2]
execsp_replicationdboption
@dbname =N'ReportServer$SQL2008R2',
@optname =N'merge publish',
```

Any command-line input or output is written as follows:

```
/SQLSVCPASSWORD="XYZ12345"
/AGTSVCACCOUNT="SSCitation\sqlagent"
/AGTSVCPASSWORD="XYZ12345"
```

New terms and **important words** are shown in bold. Words that you see on the screen, in menus or dialog boxes for example, appear in the text like this: "In the **Snapshot Agent** dialog box, check the **Create a snapshot immediately** option to apply it to the subscriber immediately."

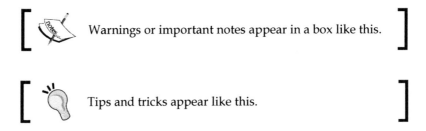

Warnings or important notes appear in a box like this.

Tips and tricks appear like this.

Reader feedback

Feedback from our readers is always welcome. Let us know what you think about this book—what you liked or may have disliked. Reader feedback is important for us to develop titles that you really get the most out of.

To send us general feedback, simply send an e-mail to feedback@packtpub.com, and mention the book title via the subject of your message.

If there is a book that you need and would like to see us publish, please send us a note in the **SUGGEST A TITLE** form on www.packtpub.com or e-mail suggest@packtpub.com.

If there is a topic that you have expertise in and you are interested in either writing or contributing to a book, see our author guide on www.packtpub.com/authors.

Customer support

Now that you are the proud owner of a Packt book, we have a number of things to help you to get the most from your purchase.

Downloading the example code for this book

You can download the example code files for all Packt books you have purchased from your account at http://www.PacktPub.com. If you purchased this book elsewhere, you can visit http://www.PacktPub.com/support and register to have the files e-mailed directly to you.

Errata

Although we have taken every care to ensure the accuracy of our content, mistakes do happen. If you find a mistake in one of our books—maybe a mistake in the text or the code—we would be grateful if you would report this to us. By doing so, you can save other readers from frustration and help us improve subsequent versions of this book. If you find any errata, please report them by visiting http://www.packtpub.com/support, selecting your book, clicking on the errata submission form link, and entering the details of your errata. Once your errata are verified, your submission will be accepted and the errata will be uploaded on our website, or added to any list of existing errata, under the Errata section of that title. Any existing errata can be viewed by selecting your title from http://www.packtpub.com/support.

Piracy

Piracy of copyright material on the Internet is an ongoing problem across all media. At Packt, we take the protection of our copyright and licenses very seriously. If you come across any illegal copies of our works, in any form, on the Internet, please provide us with the location address or website name immediately so that we can pursue a remedy.

Please contact us at copyright@packtpub.com with a link to the suspected pirated material.

We appreciate your help in protecting our authors, and our ability to bring you valuable content.

Questions

You can contact us at questions@packtpub.com if you are having a problem with any aspect of the book, and we will do our best to address it.

1
Understanding Windows Domains, Domain Users, and SQL Server Security

In this chapter, you will get an introduction to Windows domains, domain users, and SQL Server security. This will make clear and enable you to understand how the SQL Server Security mechanism works and how tightly it is integrated with the Windows domain.

In this chapter, we will learn about most important terms of Windows Servers and SQL Server, which will help us understand clustering in Windows Server as well as SQL server. We will learn about:

- What a Windows domain is and what domain users are
- Various authentication modes in Windows Server
- Authentication modes in SQL Server
- Fixed server and fixed database roles in SQL Server
- What clustering is
- What is new in SQL Server 2008
- How clustering works
- Different types of clustering in SQL Server
- Types of Quorum
- Public and private networks

Windows domains and domain users

In the early era of Windows, operating system user were created standalone until Windows NT operating system hit the market. **Windows NT**, that is, **Windows New Technology** introduced some great feature to the world — including domains.

A **domain** is a group of computers that run on Windows operating systems. Amongst them is a computer that holds all the information related to user authentication and user database and is called the **domain controller** (**server**), whereas every user who is part of this user database on the domain controller is called a **domain user**. Domain users have access to any resource across the domain and its subdomains with the privilege they have, unlike the standalone user who has access to the resources available to a specific system.

With the release of Windows Server 2000, Microsoft released Active Directory (AD), which is now widely used with Windows operating system networks to store, authenticate, and control users who are part of the domain. A Windows domain uses various modes to authenticate users — encrypted passwords, various handshake methods such as PKI, Kerberos, EAP, SSL certificates, NAP, LDAP, and IP Sec policy — and makes it robust authentication. One can choose the authentication method that suits business needs and based on the environment.

Let's now see various authentication methods in detail.

- **Public Key Infrastructure** (**PKI**): This is the most common method used to transmit data over insecure channels such as the Internet using digital certificates. It has generally two parts — the public and private keys. These keys are generated by a Certificate Authority, such as, Thawte. Public keys are stored in a directory where they are accessible by all parties. The public key is used by the message sender to send encrypted messages, which then can be decrypted using the private key.

- **Kerberos**: This is an authentication method used in client server architecture to authorize the client to use service(s) on a server in a network. In this method, when a client sends a request to use a service to a server, a request goes to the authentication server, which will generate a session key and a random value based on the username. This session key and a random value are then passed to the server, which grants or rejects the request. These sessions are for certain time period, which means for that particular amount of time the client can use the service without having to re-authenticate itself.

- **Extensible Authentication Protocol** (**EAP**): This is an authentication protocol generally used in wireless and point-to-point connections.

- **SSL Certificates**: A Secure Socket Layer certificate (SSL) is a digital certificate that is used to identify a website or server that provides a service to clients and sends the data in an encrypted form. SSL certificates are typically used by websites such as GMAIL. When we type a URL and press *Enter*, the web browser sends a request to the web server to identify itself. The web server then sends a copy of its SSL certificate, which is checked by the browser. If the browser trusts the certificate (this is generally done on the basis of the CA and Registration Authority and directory verification), it will send a message back to the server and in reply the web server sends an acknowledgement to the browser to start an encrypted session.

- **Network Access Protection (NAP)**: This is a new platform introduced by Microsoft with the release of Windows Server 2008. It will provide access to the client, based on the identity of the client, the group it belongs to, and the level compliance it has with the policy defined by the Network Administrators. If the client doesn't have a required compliance level, NAP has mechanisms to bring the client to the compliance level dynamically and allow it to access the network.

- **Lightweight Directory Access Protocol (LDAP)**: This is a protocol that runs over TCP/IP directly. It is a set of objects, that is, organizational units, printers, groups, and so on. When the client sends a request for a service, it queries the LDAP server to search for availability of information, and based on that information and level of access, it will provide access to the client.

- **IP Security (IPSEC)**: IP Security is a set of protocols that provides security at the network layer. IP Sec provides two choices:
  - **Authentication Header**: Here it encapsulates the authentication of the sender in a header of the network packet.
  - **Encapsulating Security Payload**: Here it supports encryption of both the header and data.

Now that we know basic information on Windows domains, domain users, and various authentication methods used with Windows servers, I will walk you through some of the basic and preliminary stuff about SQL Server security!

Understanding SQL Server Security

Security!! Now-a-days we store various kinds of information into databases and we just want to be sure that they are secured. Security is the most important word to the IT administrator and vital for everybody who has stored their information in a database as he/she needs to make sure that not a single piece of data should be made available to someone who shouldn't have access. Because all the information stored in the databases is vital, everyone wants to prevent unauthorized access to highly confidential data and here is how security implementation in SQL Server comes into the picture.

With the release of SQL Server 2000, Microsoft (MS) has introduced some great security features such as authentication roles (fixed server roles and fixed database roles), application roles, various permissions levels, forcing protocol encryption, and so on, which are widely used by administrators to tighten SQL Server security.

Basically, SQL Server security has two paradigms: one is SQL Server's own set of security measures and other is to integrate them with the domain. SQL Server has two methods of authentication.

Windows authentication

In Windows authentication mode, we can integrate domain accounts to authenticate users, and based on the group they are members of and level of access they have, DBAs can provide them access on the particular SQL server box.

Whenever a user tries to access the SQL Server, his/her account is validated by the domain controller first, and then based on the permission it has, the domain controller allows or rejects the request; here it won't require separate login ID and password to authenticate. Once the user is authenticated, SQL server will allow access to the user based on the permission it has. These permissions are in form of Roles including Server, fixed DB Roles, and Application roles.

- **Fixed Server Roles**: These are security principals that have server-wide scope. Basically, fixed server roles are expected to manage the permissions at server level. We can add SQL logins, domain accounts, and domain groups to these roles. There are different roles that we can assign to a login, domain account, or group—the following table lists them.

Role name	Permission user can have
Sysadmin	Can perform any activity in the server
Serveradmin	Can change server-wide configuration and shut down server
Securityadmin	Can manage logins and their properties
Processadmin	Can end the process that are running in SQL Server
Setupadmin	Can add or remove linked servers
Bulkadmin	Can run the bulk insert statement
Diskadmin	Can manage the disk files
Dbcreator	Can create, alter, drop, or restore any database
public	Default role assigned to each login

- **Fixed DB Roles**: These are the roles that are assigned to a particular login for the particular database; its scope is limited to the database it has permission to. There are various fixed database roles, including the ones shown in the following table:

Role name	Permission user has
db_accessadmin	Alter any users, create schema, connect
db_backupoperator	Back up database, log, and create checkpoint
db_datareader	Can execute select statement
db_datawriter	Can execute delete, insert, and update statements
db_ddladmin	alter — assembly, asymmetric key, certificate, database DDL trigger, database event, notification, dataspace, fulltext catalog, message type, remote server binding, route, schema, service, symmetric key, checkpoint; create — aggregate, default, function, procedure, queue, rule, synonym, table, table, view, XML schema collection and references
db_denydatareader	Cannot execute select
db_denydatawriter	The role is to revoke the right/permission for select statement
db_owner	Can perform any action in the database
db_securityadmin	Can alter — application role, any role, create schema, view definition
dbm_monitor	Can view most recent status in database mirroring monitor

- **Application Role**: The Application role is a database principal that is widely used to assign user permissions for an application. For example, in a home-grown ERP, some users require only to view the data; we can create a role and add a `db_datareader` permission to it and then can add all those users who require read-only permission.

- **Mixed authentication**: In the Mixed authentication mode, logins can be authenticated by the Windows domain controller or by SQL Server itself. DBAs can create logins with passwords in SQL Server. With the release of SQL Server 2005, MS has introduced `password` policies for SQL Server logins. Mixed mode authentication is used when one has to run a legacy application and it is not on the domain network.

In my opinion, Windows authentication is good because we can use various handshake methods such as PKI, Kerberos, EAP, SSL NAP, LDAP, or IPSEC to tighten the security.

SQL Server 2005 has enhancements in its security mechanisms. The most important features amongst them are password policy, native encryption, separation of users and schema, and no need to provide system administrator (SA) rights to run profiler.

These are good things because SA is the super user, and with the power this account has, a user can do anything on the SQL box, including:

- The user can grant ALTER TRACE permission to users who require to run profiler
- The user can create login and users
- The user can grant or revoke permission to other users

A schema is an object container that is owned by a user and is transferable to any other users. In earlier versions, objects are owned by users, so if the user leaves the company we cannot delete his/her account from the SQL box just because there is some object he/she has created. We first have to change the owner of that object and then we can delete that account. On the other hand, in the case of a schema, we could have dropped the user account because the object is owned by the schema.

Now, SQL Server 2008 will give you more control over the configuration of security mechanisms. It allows you to configure metadata access, execution context, and auditing events using DDL triggers — the most powerful feature to audit any DDL event.

If one wishes to know more about what we have seen till now, he/she can go through the following links:

- `http://www.microsoft.com/sqlserver/2008/en/us/Security.aspx`
- `http://www.microsoft.com/sqlserver/2005/en/us/security-features.aspx`
- `http://technet.microsoft.com/en-us/library/cc966507.aspx`

In this section, we understood the basics of domains, domain users, and SQL Server security. We also learned why security is given so much emphasize these days.

In the next section, we will understand the basics of clustering and its components.

What is clustering?

Before starting with SQL Server clustering, let's have a look at clustering in general and Windows clusters.

The word **Cluster** itself is self-descriptive—a bunch or group. When two or more than two computers are connected to each other by means of a network and share some of the common resources to provide redundancy or performance improvement, they are known as a cluster of computers.

Clustering is usually deployed when there is a critical business application running that needs to be available 24 X 7 or in terminology—High Availability. These clusters are known as Failover clusters because the primary goal to set up the cluster is to make services or business processes that are business critical available 24 X 7. MS Windows server Enterprise and Datacenter edition supports failover clustering. This is achieved by having two identical nodes connected to each other by means of private network or commonly used resources. In case of failure of any common resource or services, the first node (**Active**) passes the ownership to another node (**Passive**).

SQL Server Clustering is built on top of Windows Clustering, which means before we go about installing SQL Server clustering, we should have Windows clustering installed. Before we start, let's understand the commonly used shared resources for the cluster server.

Clusters with 2, 4, 8, 12 or 32 nodes can be built Windows Server 2008 R2. Clusters are categorized in the following manner:

- **High-Availability Clusters**:

  This type of cluster is known as a Failover cluster. High Availability clusters are implemented when the purpose is to provide highly available services.

For implementing a failover or high availability cluster one may have up to 16 nodes in a Microsoft Cluster. Clustering in Windows operating systems was first introduced with the release of Windows NT 4.0 Enterprise Edition, and was enhanced gradually. Even though we can have non-identical hardware, we should use identical hardware. This is because if the node to which cluster fails over has lower configuration, then we might face degradation in performance.

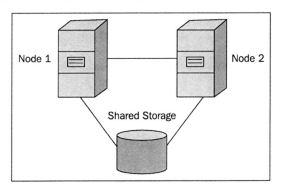

- **Load Balancing**:

  This is the second form of cluster that can be configured. This type of cluster can be configured by linking multiple computers with each other and making use of each resource they need for operation. From the user's point of view, all of these servers/nodes linked to each other are different. However, it is collectively and virtually a single system, with the main goal being to balance work by sharing CPU, disk, and every possible resource among the linked nodes and that is why it is known as a Load Balancing cluster.

   [SQL Server doesn't support this form of clustering.]

- **Compute Clusters**:

  When computers are linked together with the purpose of using them for simulation for aircraft, they are known as a compute cluster. A well-known example is Beowulf computers.

- **Grid Computing**:

  This is one kind of clustering solution, but it is more often used when there is a dispersed location. This kind of cluster is called a Supercomputer or HPC. The main application is scientific research, academic, mathematical, or weather forecasting where lots of CPUs and disks are required—SETI@home is a well-known example.

If we talk about SQL Server clusters, there are some cool new features that are added in the latest release of SQL Server 2008, although with the limitation that these features are available only if SQL Server 2008 is used with Windows Server 2008. So, let's have a glance at these features:

- ○ **Service SID**: Service SIDs were introduced with Windows Vista and Windows Server 2008. They enable us to bind permissions directly to Windows services. In the earlier version of SQL Server 2005, we need to have a SQL Server Services account that is a member of a domain group so that it can have all the required permissions. This is not the case with SQL Server 2008 and we may choose Service SIDs to bypass the need to provision domain groups.

- ○ **Support for 16 nodes**: We may add up to 16 nodes in our SQL Server 2008 cluster with SQL Server 2008 Enterprise 64-bit edition.

- ○ **New cluster validation**: As a part of the installation steps, a new cluster validation step is implemented. Prior to adding a node into an existing cluster, this validation step checks whether or not the cluster environment is compatible.

- ○ **Mount Drives**: Drive letters are no longer essential. If we have a cluster configured that has limited drive letters available, we may mount a drive and use it in our cluster environment, provided it is associated with the base drive letter.

- ○ **Geographically dispersed cluster node**: This is the super-cool feature introduced with SQL Server 2008, which uses VLAN to establish connectivity with other cluster nodes. It breaks the limitation of having all clustered nodes at a single location.

- ○ **IPv6 Support**: SQL Server 2008 natively supports IPv6, which increases network IP address size to 128 bit from 32 bit.

- ○ **DHCP Support**: Windows server 2008 clustering introduced the use of DHCP-assigned IP addresses by the cluster services and it is supported by SQL Server 2008 clusters. It is recommended to use static IP addresses. This is because if some of our application depends on IP addresses, or in case of failure of renewing IP address from DHCP server, there would be a failure of IP address resources.

- ○ **iSCSI Support**: Windows server 2008 supports iSCSI to be used as storage connection; in earlier versions, only SAN and fibre channels were supported.

How clustering works

A highly available application or system is the key concept in cluster environment. Microsoft SQL Server is a cluster-aware application, and it works well to cater for this business need. Let's see how it works.

Before we go further into details, let's see some common terms here:

- **Active/Passive Cluster**: In this setup, there will be one server that remains idle and takes over the control or the ownership of the resources at the time of failover.
- **Active/Active Cluster**: Here, the only difference is that both the nodes in the cluster are active and running, and the surviving node will take over the control or the ownership of the resources when a failover occurs.
- **Public Network**: This is a network available to external resources or systems.
- **Private Network aka Heartbeat**: This is a network that is available to SQL Server cluster nodes only; heartbeat is used to check the health of another node.
- **Shared Disk Array**: A disk array is nothing but more than one disk used collectively and shared among the cluster nodes. However, at any point of time only one node — the active node or the owner of the resources — can access the disks, in order to protect data from being overwritten.
- **Quorum**: This is the disk resource wherein the status of the cluster is being written, especially by the Windows clustering. Failure of this resource can lead to failure of the entire clustering setup.
- **Cluster Name**: This is the name of a Windows cluster.
- **Cluster IP**: This refers to the IP address on the public network that is used by external systems or client machines to connect to the cluster.
- **Cluster Resource Type**: This can be any resource that can be configured for clustering, that is, a physical disk.
- **Cluster Account**: This is the Administrator account used to control and run the services for a cluster; this account must be configured at the domain level and should be added to the local administrator group in each cluster node.
- **Cluster Group**: This is a kind of container, for example, SQL Server, wherein cluster-aware applications or services are grouped.
- **Cluster Name for Virtual SQL Server**: This is the name of a Virtual SQL Server, which is then used by client machines to connect to.
- **IP for Virtual SQL Server**: This will be the IP address used by SQL Server, and clients use this IP address to connect to SQL Server.
- **Full-text Search**: SQL Server Full-Text search.

MSDTC

Microsoft Distributed Transaction Coordinator (**MSDTC**) is a service used by the SQL Server when it is required to have distributed transactions between more than one machine. In a clustered environment, SQL Server service can be hosted on any of the available nodes if the active node fails, and in this case MSDTC comes into the picture in case we have distributed queries and for replication, and hence the MSDTC service should be running.

As we have understood the basics of the components that are used while working with clustering, let's now have a look at how it actually works.

Let's see the example of a Single Node failover cluster. Here, in this case, if anything goes wrong with the active node, the second node will become active and take over the control and ownership of the resources. It is recommended to use fibre channel or SCSI cables for the shared disk arrays for each node. Also, the data should be stored on the shared disk so that it will become accessible by both the nodes in case of failure; however, please note that at any given time only one node can access the disk, in order to protect the data from being overwritten. Apart from these considerations, select a disk system that supports fault tolerance, that is, a RAID array.

So the question arises as to how the passive node senses the failure. Recollect that we just talked about the public and private network (Heartbeat). The public network is exposed to the external resources or computers whereas the private network is shared between cluster nodes. What happens here is, whenever a service or resource gets stressed out or doesn't respond to the private network, that is, its Heartbeat fails, node2 or the passive node initiates the process to take over the ownership of the resources owned by node1. We can refer to the following image:

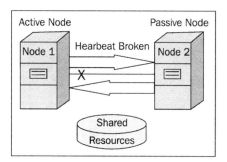

There are some questions that could be asked. Let's now have a look at some of the main questions:

- **Question**: What will happen to the data that is being accessed?

  Answer: Well, this is taken care of by shared disk arrays as it is shared and every node that is part of the cluster can access it; however, one node at a time can access and own it.

- **Question**: What about clients that were connected previously? Does the failover mean that developers will have to modify the connection string?

  Answer: Nothing like this happens. SQL Server is installed as a virtual server and it has a virtual IP address and that too is shared by every cluster node. So, the client actually knows only one SQL Server or its IP address. Here are the steps that explain how Failover will work:

  - Node 1 owns the resources as of now, and is active node.
  - The network adapter driver gets corrupted or suffers a physical damage.
  - Heartbeat between Node1 and Node 2 is broken.
  - Node 2 initiates the process to take ownership of the resources owned by the Node 1.
  - It would approximately take two to five minutes to complete the process.

There are mainly two ways that inform whether a failover should occur.

- **Heartbeat**: We have just seen this in the preceding example.
- **Resource-specific detection**: Almost every resource that is part of a cluster has its own specific method such as SQL Server Service, Analysis service, disks, and so on:

  - **SQL Server and Analysis service**: These rely on the network name and IP address. If any of this fails, SQL Server or Analysis service goes offline.
  - **Shared Disks**: There are vendor-provided applications that are cluster-aware and which will check periodically whether or not the resource is available.

Windows server has built-in support called `LooksAlive`, to check every five seconds whether or not the services are running. How it works is, after every five seconds, `SOAGTRES.DLL`, a resource DLL that runs under the cluster account service context, makes a call to the service control manager to check a registry entry to be sure that it is running and sends acknowledgement back to `SOAGTRES.DLL` as either true or false.

IsAlive (which occurs every 60 seconds) is a more detailed detection performed by the SQSRVRES.DLL that does the task of verifying that SQL resources are online, registry entries are correct, and SQL Server is running in normal mode. It also checks if the system databases are running normally by executing T-SQL. The IsAlive check internally calls Resource Monitor, which reports the status of resources to SQLSRVRES.DLL, as either 0 (false) or 1 (true). Resource Monitor depends on the registry for the status information. The status information is compared with the cached value in cluster configuration database; if Resource Monitor returns the status as offline/offline pending, failed, or false, then SQLSRVRES.DLL will call the Online function to bring the resource back online. If it doesn't succeed in the retries (here it executes select @@servername), it finally considers that particular resource as failed and sends it back to Resource Monitor. In turn, this triggers the failover process with the help of the failover manager. If the resource becomes online in the first attempt, or within the retries limit, the failover process doesn't occur; on the other hand, if the resource fails to become online and exceeds the limit of retries, the failover process is initiated.

Types of clusters

There are four types of clustering solutions available with SQL Server 2008, which are the following:

- Failover Cluster: Single-instance Cluster
- Failover Cluster: Multi-instance Cluster
    ◦ All nodes with active instances
    ◦ N+1
- Failover Cluster: Multi-site Cluster
- Failover Cluster: Guest Cluster

Single-instance Cluster

This is the most common and widely used architecture for configuring SQL Server clusters. In this type of clustering, there will be two participating nodes in which one will be active or owner of the resources and the second will be passive. Whenever something crashes or fails, the active node passes ownership of all the resources to the second node — this is called failover.

As there is only a single node that is active or holds a resource like SQL Server services in running mode, this type of clustering is called Single-instance Clustering.

Note: There is a misconception that I often see with the terms **Active/Active** and **Active/Passive**. Let me clarify the terms here, and illustrate why the cluster is being referred to as Active/Passive or Active/Active; however, in any case both are possible with Single-Instance Clusters only.

The most common and widely used configuration is called an Active/Passive cluster (Single-instance Failover Cluster). There will be two nodes that are configured as a cluster node, and one of them is active and the second will remain passive or idle. In case of failure of any kind on Node 1, it fails over to second (or passive) server and now Node 2 will become the primary or active node for the cluster. Refer to the following scenario. If there is a failure in the active node the **Heartbeat** (refer to the *How clustering works* section) will be interrupted and ownership of the any resources will be taken by Node 2, which was passive:

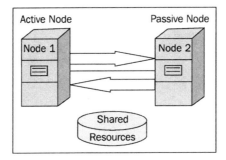

Multi-instance Cluster

In this type of clustering, there can be more than one node failover. This means in case of failure there can be more than one node actively available to take over the ownership of the resources.

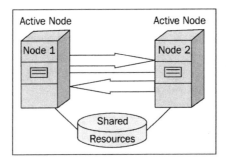

As its name says, there will be one or more than one instance or node running in the failover cluster. In the first type of configuration all the nodes are equal. When a node fails, all the failover instances will fail over to another node. What we should remember here is that we need to tolerate multiple node failures. The reason is simple: the node that will take over the ownership should be capable enough of serving the peak hours work load. And, for this, we should use `AntiAffinityClassNames` to set priority.

The second type of configuration is referred to as n+1. In this type of cluster, there will be a dedicated node available to take on the workload of any other node in case of failure. This configuration increases capacity when all nodes are available, in other words—optimum utilization of resources. We may also have an option to limit the number of dedicated nodes within the total limit of nodes that the SQL Server clustering solution supports. To have better control over instance allocation during failover or balancing, we should use preferred owner or `AntiAffinityClassNames` on the resource group.

In this type of configuration, there will be two nodes that are active and so it can be called a multi-instance cluster. This means that at any given point there will be two separate SQL Server instances running in a clustered environment. In case of failure (say Node 1 fails), all the users, applications, or database(s) that are connected to Node 1 will start using Node 2 and its resources. So, here it is more important to consider that the load might increase on Node 2 while designing or sizing, such as setting minimum and maximum memory; leaving default settings for minimum and maximum memory will consume all available memory and release memory to the OS as and when required, which is not desired. We can refer to the following screenshot.

Multi-site Failover Cluster

This was introduced in SQL Server 2005 clustering, and is also known as **geographically dispersed failover** or **stretch cluster** as it is designed to cope with the situation of a disaster at one site. This is how it functions: There are two sites at physically dispersed locations or sites or datacenters. If there is damage or failure at one site, the other will be up and running, providing a much more robust solution and high availability.

We can refer to the following screenshot:

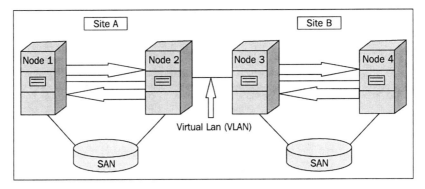

There are six things you should not forget when you decide to use multi-site clustering:

- Our data should get replicated consistently and continuously on the other site. This will ensure that we have the latest data and can tolerate disk failover. If our database and logs are on separate disk drives, we need to ensure that they both get replicated to avoid any data losses and maintain consistency in the state of the data.

- Use Stretch VLAN so that a single subnet masks across all the participating nodes. Windows Server 2008 Cluster supports different subnet masks across cluster nodes; the same feature is yet to be added to SQL Server 2008. Most of the data centers at different locations do not share a single subnet, and it is necessary to have single subnet to have connectivity between these sites.

- Quorum should be configured in a way that either site would run in case of failure of the other. The configuration of the Quorum is the same as it is with single-site failover.

- Heartbeat configuration is supposed to tolerate increased latency; this can be achieved by increasing latency in the Windows server failover cluster inter-node heartbeat so that it does not detect it as stress.

- Ensure that the disk resources are a part of the same group, and there are no non-disk resource dependencies to any of the disks. By default, Node and Disk Majority mode is selected, and in the case of odd number of nodes, Node Majority is selected.

- Having a single subnet will ensure that the store replication and clustering between two geographically dispersed locations is similar to a single-site failover cluster.

Guest Failover Clustering

Guest Failover Clustering is nothing but installing and configuring clustering using virtual machines. In guest failover configuration you may have the cluster nodes on the same physical server, although it is recommended that you configure cluster nodes on different physical servers. The reason is that you will run in to pain when there is damage in the physical box; so to have the application or database available you must configure cluster nodes on separate physical nodes.

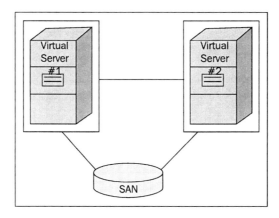

Both the versions, SQL Server 2005 and SQL Server 2008, support Guest Failover Clustering. The pre-requisites are:

- The host operating system should be running on a supported virtualization environment such as:
  - Windows Server 2008 with Hyper-V
  - Microsoft Hyper-V server 2008
  - Certified configuration from Server Virtualization Validation Program (SVVP)

- The guest operating system should be running on Windows Server 2008.

- The environment should meet the requirements mentioned in the knowledge-based article at http://support.microsoft.com/kb/943984.

Components of clustering

There are some components that we need to carefully consider before we go about designing cluster architecture and installing. Here are the components:

Shared disk array

As the name implies, the disks are shared. The reason behind using shared disk arrays is the fact that they are accessible from remote locations or clients and this is exactly what is required by cluster services.

The cluster architecture forces us to use shared disk resources, as the disk to be used with the cluster environment should be accessible by any of the nodes. The shared disk plays a vital role in the cluster, because it stores not only data files, but logs, FILESTREAM files, and full-text index files. In case of failover, the preferred node will have access and ownership for the disk resource so that clients can access the database system without any interruption.

The shared disk should be reliable and fault tolerant as it stores database files. We can have this shared disk resource in form of Fibre Channel SCSI or SAN.

Internet Small Computer System Interface

In the earlier version of SCSI, we needed to set special cabling, which we need not worry about in the **Internet Small Computer System Interface (iSCSI)** as it works well with IP and that is the beauty of the iSCSI—it is used to transfer data across intranets and to manage storage for long distances. This feature is really very useful and handy in the case of Multi-site clustering because we may use it as a location-independent storage solution.

Also, administrators can consider using iSCSI from the point of view of storage consolidation, that is, dispersed located data center, or multi-site clustering, among others.

Storage Area Network (SAN)

SAN is network storage, which is meant to be used when we need to consolidate our storage at our corporate network or at our data center as a highly reliable storage solution.

SAN has multiple (sometimes hundreds of) hard disks attached to it using high performance adapters. Also, it has a great caching capacity that increases the performance ultimately. All these hard disk drives are then virtualized or created logically thus labeled as **Logical Unit Number (LUN)**. These LUNs can be shared or dedicated to a particular application, such as, SQL Server.

Every operating system maintains its own file system to the dedicated LUNs, that is, NTFS, and when it comes to shared LUNs among different flavors of operating systems, it may use SAN File systems to cater to the need. In most cases, SAN uses fibre channel to connect to the network, called Fibre Channel over Ethernet (FCoE), though it is not limited to FCoE only.

Redundant Array of Independent Disks

Redundant Array of Independent Disks (RAID) provides better fault-tolerance by making use of redundancy of disk(s). RAIDs are widely used as storage solutions to get the best I/O performance, based on the application, whether the application is write intensive or read intensive. We may have a choice having RAID array with iSCSI or SAN. There are mainly three concepts in RAID:

- **Mirroring**: In this type, an entire disk is mirrored on another disk or set of disks using hardware or software-level mirroring. Mirroring creates a replica of what is written on one disk on another disk, or set of disks, and that is why configuring Mirroring requires at least two drives, for example, RAID 1.

- **Striping**: Here, there are two or more disks required to configure striping. While writing data into disks or reading from the disks, it is spread across all the disks configured in stripes and thus gives best performance for writing as each disk has its own reader, for example, RAID 5.

- **Parity**: In general, parity sets status as even or odd by adding a bit known as the parity bit. For even parity, the parity bit is set to 1 if the number of ones in the set of bits (not including the parity bit) is odd. On the other hand for odd parity, the parity bit is set to 1 if the number of ones is even. So, if there is some corruption in data being written or read, it will not match the pattern and thus reports incorrect status, for example, RAID 5. This is generally known as *fault-tolerance*.

There are many RAID arrays available such as RAID 0, RAID 1, RAID 3, RAID 4, RAID 5, RAID 6, RAID 10, and RAID 01. Here, we will discuss only those that are widely used with the SQL Server to boost performance level.

- **RAID1**: This is the simplest form of RAID array. It requires a minimum of two disks to create a RAID1 array. RAID1 creates a replica of the disk being written, and is extremely helpful to recover data in case of physical damage to the first disk. RAID1 is the perfect choice to store operating systems, binaries, and database log files.

- **RAID5**: RAID5, also known as *stripe set with parity,* requires three or more disks, and it creates and stores parity values internally. So in case of failure or damage of a single disk, data can be recalculated and rebuilt on a newly added drive. Please be aware that this will degrade the performance until the disk that has failed or damaged is rebuilt. This type of RAID is most useful when our application is read intensive as it reads data in a sequential manner.

- **RAID10**: RAID10 is also known as *mirrored stripe* or *mirrored then striped.* This means it is a combination of RAID1+RAID0. RAID10 is used when we want best performance with a write-intensive application or data files and tempdb, as it writes data in a random manner.

The Quorum

Dictionary says that a **Quorum** is the minimum number that should match to perform a task further or to make a decision. Here, in the case of clustering, the meaning is no different.

As we all know by now, the cluster nodes send and receive information over the network. It is very possible that sometimes a change is done at the node that is the owner or active node, which then fails before sending the data back to another node in the cluster; in this case the cluster will not work. The nodes in clusters vote and based on that it will be decided whether or not the node should continue; for example, there is a four-node cluster and three of them can talk to each other but not the node3.

Quorum is a resource where all events pertaining to SQL Server Clusters get logged or recorded on a separate disk. Events can include change in the configuration, in active node, or owner of the resources changed, among others.

With SQL Server 2008, Microsoft has made significant changes, which will help easily create Quorum on the basis of its application and to do so automatically. There are four types of quorum available, including:

- **Node Majority**: In this mode, each cluster node can vote. Majority is decided upon 50 percent of the nodes. If votes come for 50 percent or greater than 50 percent, then the cluster will function. This is the preferred selection when there is no shared disk or storage provided and numbers of nodes are odd. Consider an example where a three-node cluster is set up. Now if one of the nodes fails to communicate, what will happen? In this case, the votes will be more than 50 percent as two out of three nodes are functioning and communicating with each other and that is why it will continue to function. On the contrary, if only one node is functioning properly of the three, then the cluster will fail to work.

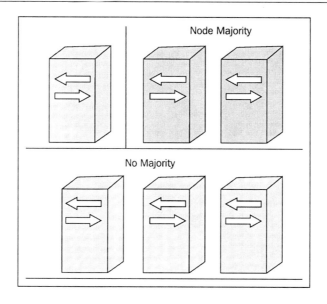

- **Node and Disk Majority**: In this configuration, every cluster node plus a designated disk (as a witness) can vote, and here too if more than 50 percent votes are calculated to keep running as a cluster, the cluster will continue to function. This means if there is a four-node cluster with a disk witness, the total number of disks adds up to five as there are four disks on the system plus one witness disk; so, in this case, the cluster will continue to work if three or more votes come.

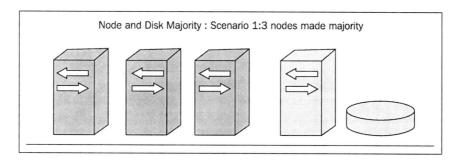

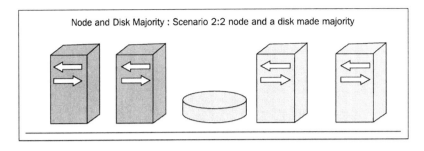

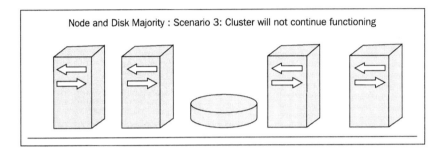

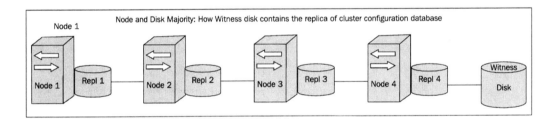

This configuration is recommended where there is a two-node failover cluster or there is an even-node cluster configured. Please note that while configuring an even number of nodes, if the wizard automatically selects Node and Disk Majority, it will also select a witness disk. The wizard also considers selecting the smallest size disk of more than 512MB as a witness disk.

Keep the following things in mind while implementing this configuration:

○ Use a small LUN that has a minimum size of 512 MB.

○ Make sure that this disk is dedicated to be the disk witness and contains no user data.

○ It is not required to assign a drive letter to this LUN; we can decide this based on our cluster need.

- This LUN should be a single volume and should be added as a cluster resource.

- Ensure that this LUN is validated and configured using hardware RAID and is formatted using the NTFS file system.

- **Node and File share majority**: In this mode, there will be a designated file share that is created as a file share witness. There will be a replica for each of the shares, which is kept on a system disk across all the nodes; however, this is not stored on the file share, which is the core difference between *node and disk majority* and *disk and file share majority*.

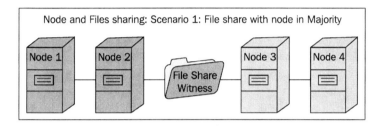

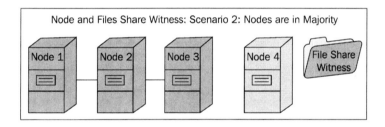

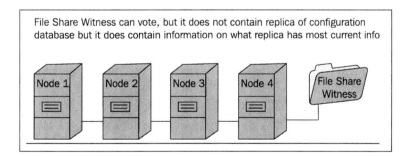

This file share keeps an eye on each of the disks so it knows which has the most up-to-date replica. This configuration is recommended in a geographically dispersed failover cluster.

Keep the following in mind while implementing this configuration:

- ° Use **Server Message Block (SMB)**.
- ° Ensure that the file share has a minimum 5 MB of free space.
- ° The file share should be dedicated to the cluster.
- ° It should not be on a server that is a cluster node or would become cluster node in future — file server would be a good choice.
- ° The file share should be on the same forest of the domain.
- ° Ensure that the administrator has the full permission for the share and NTFS.

- **No majority – Disk only**: This mode of Quorum is similar to the previous versions of Quorum with Windows Server 2003. This is recommended in only selected configurations. This is because in this case, if a single disk fails, then entire cluster will fail.

  The cluster replica will help here as it stores the exact and most up-to-date replica of the cluster database on the shared disk, which is accessible by all the nodes. In case of failure of a single node, this replica is considered as an authoritative replica to help repair or replace the Quorum that has been corrupted or damaged.

Once the configuration for the Quorum is over and we want to have a look at it, there are two options: we may either open a GUI (a cluster management snap-in) or use the command prompt by typing `Cluster / quorum`.

When it comes to making changes to existing Quorum configuration, we may do it using:

- Failover cluster management snap-in
- Managing a cluster
- Action
- More action
- Configuring cluster Quorum settings
- Following the wizard the way we want our Quorum to be configured

Public and Private Network

In a clustering, each cluster node or every node that is a candidate for being a cluster node should have two Network Interface Cards (NICs) as a base requirement — one card can be used to configure the Public Network and second can be used to configure the Private Network.

- **Public Network**: In a clustering environment, a network that is exposed to the public, that is, client systems to connect to is called the Public Network.

- **Private Network**: A network that is used to connect two or more cluster nodes is known as the Private Network, also known as the Heartbeat.

  SQL Server uses this Heartbeat network for health detection between two or more nodes, especially in a single-node failover cluster. Consider a situation where we have configured a single-node failover cluster—Node1 and Node2. Node1 is holding ownership of the cluster resources and Node2 is in passive mode and has no access to or ownership of any cluster resources.

  In case of failure or unmanaged shutdown, or for any reason if Node1 is rebooted or shut down, the Private Network or Heartbeat between these two nodes fails and the Node2 of the cluster will become the active node. It will now have ownership of and access to all the cluster resources until it fails over to Node1.

  SQL Server MVP Brad McGehee, in his article, has mentioned some excellent points that should be considered while configuring the Public and Private Networks. The article can be found at `http://www.sql-server-perform-ance.com/articles/clustering/cluster_infrastructure_p1.aspx`.

Summary

In this chapter, we have learned about clustering in general and what clustering in Windows and SQL Server means. We have also learned some of the new features introduced with SQL Server 2008.

We learned about Public and Private Networks in clustering, their significance, and how they function in SQL Server clustering. We also looked at some of the things that need to be considered before we go about configuring a network for our cluster nodes. We saw different types of clusters such as Single-Failover Cluster, Multi-Failover Cluster, Multi-site Failover Cluster, and Guest Failover Cluster. We also saw different types of disk storage that can be used while configuring clusters, along with the most important part of a cluster, Quorum.

In the next chapter, we will learn what the prerequisites for SQL Server Cluster installation are and how to install SQL Server Cluster using a wizard and T-SQL.

2
Implementing Clustering

One fine morning, Mr. Young, who is an IT Manager at XY Incorporation, received a call from his office, asking him to rush to the office immediately, as the database server that the office uses as their production database had crashed.

Mr. Young reached the office and started restoring data from the last full database backup, followed by the incremental backup, and then Transaction log backup to recover all data lost to the point. SQL Server allows taking backups of transaction logs if the SQL Server Engine can read transaction log files, and this type of Transaction log backup is known as **Tail Log** backup. When Mr. Young tried to take a Tail Log backup, the log file was so corrupt that he could not take a Tail Log backup. To add to it, the last Transaction Log file backup was taken 10 minutes before the server crashed and hence Mr. Young ended up losing 10 minutes of data. Restoring the database and pointing business application and websites took four hours and it was a big loss to the company. In the board meeting, Mr. Young finally came up with the research plan and proposal which, when implemented, would help them avoid such circumstances in the future. Although this solution was a little costly, the company approved the proposal and asked him to implement SQL Server Cluster. Let's see how SQL Server Cluster would help him and how he implemented it.

As we have mentioned in the previous chapter, a cluster is basically a group of two or more servers, known as nodes, that can work together. Clustering allows a node to take over the control of services and/or resources of another node in the case of physical damage or failure of that node. Clustering is the most suitable option to make a database(s) highly available, when it is required to configure them on every server.

In this chapter, we will take a look at the installation procedure for **single node failover cluster**, that is, **Active/Passive**, and **Multi-instance Failover Cluster**, that is, **Active/Active**. We will realize that a lot of changes have been implemented, when we compare the installation of a cluster on Windows Server 2003 environment with SQL Server 2005 to installing a cluster on Windows Server 2008 with SQL Server 2008—for example, Quorum is now known as Witness Disks. Moreover, there are some changes that we may encounter when we install clustering on Windows 2008 R2, the step-by-step installation wizard covering the following:

- Preparing for clustering
- Validating
- Installing a cluster

What is Hyper-V?

Let's now see what the Hyper-V is:

- It is a hypervisor-based technology that allows multiple operating systems to run on a host operating system at the same time. It has advantages of using SQL Server 2008 R2 on Windows Server 2008 R2 with Hyper-V. One such example could be the ability to migrate a live server, thereby increasing high availability without incurring downtime, among others.

- Hyper-V now supports up to 64 logical processors.

- It can host up to four VMs on a single licensed host server. SQL Server 2008 R2 allows an unrestricted number of virtual servers, thus making consolidation easy.

- It has the ability to manage multiple SQL Servers centrally using **Utility Control Point (UCP)**.

- Sysprep utility can be used to create preconfigured VMs so that SQL Server deployment becomes easier.

 There are two more words that are commonly used to refer to Virtual Machines, namely, Sandbox and **Virtual PC (VPC)**. So, we shouldn't be confused if we encounter words such as VM, Sandbox, or VPC—they represent the same thing.

All these features make it easier to understand and implement Windows Server 2008 clustering.

Installation prerequisites for SQL Server 2008 R2

Let's drive through the installation prerequisites for SQL Server 2008 R2 clustering on Windows Server 2008 R2 Enterprise Edition. We will cover the following prerequisites:

- Hardware and software requirements
- Operating system
- Server role and feature
- IP addresses
- Network name
- Shared disks
- Security

Hardware requirements

The following are the hardware requirements:

- Intel Xeon Quad Core 3430 2.4GHz CPU
- 4 GB ECC RDIMM DDR3 RAM @ 1333, 8 MB Shared L3 Cache
- Intel S3420GPLC Server Board, 500 GB SATA HDD

 We should use Microsoft Certified hardware. We can find the list of all tested products at http://www.windowsservercatalog.com/ and a KB article http://support.microsoft.com/kb/309395.

Software requirements

The following are the software requirements:

- Windows Server 2008 R2 Enterprise Edition with Hyper-V
- SQL Server 2008 R2 November CTP
- StarWind iSCSI Server 5.2.1090.0

Operating system requirements

To install SQL Server 2008 clustering, it's essential to have Windows Server 2008 Enterprise or Data Center Edition installed on our host system with Full Installation, so that we don't have to go back and forth and install the required components and restart the system.

Server role and feature

As Windows clustering requires a cluster node to be a member of **Active Directory Services (ADS)**, it is a must that we install Active Directory Services. Now, ADS depends on the **Internet Information Services** (IIS) and **Directory Naming Services** (**DNS**), so it is required to install these too.

With the release of Windows Server 2008, MS has introduced something called Server Role and Feature. Here, in order to be a member of a cluster, a node should have Application Role installed. This, in turn, installs .NET framework 3.5.1 and Distributed Transaction Services, which must be installed prior to installing SQL Server cluster.

Along with the Server roles mentioned above, we should install the Failover clustering feature before attempting to install the SQL Server 2008 cluster.

Please make a note that only Application Role, DTS, and Failover clustering features need to be installed on both the nodes, whereas ADS, DNS, and IIS need to be installed on **Domain Controller (DC)**.

IP addresses

Although Windows Server 2008 R2 supports cluster nodes to use DHCP address, we will use static address. The reason to use static IP address is that SQL Server 2008 clustering still doesn't support DHCP addresses.

 Please refer to the *Public and private network* section in *Chapter 1, Understanding Windows Domain, Domain Users, and SQL Server Security*.

We should procure one IP address for Windows Cluster, SQL Server Cluster, and MSDTC each, and two IP addresses for each member node—in our case, it's two nodes that are participating, so four IP addresses. We also need one IP address for a public network (a network that is known to client computers) and one IP for a private network (a network that is known by the cluster nodes only for the quick health detection called Heart Beat Signal). This means all-in-all we need to have seven IP addresses while clustering.

Name of resources	Number of IP addresses
Private Network, that is, Heart Beat (one per node)	2
Public Network (one per node)	2
MSDTC	1
Windows Cluster Name	1
SQL Server Cluster Name	1

In case we are installing a Multi-instance Failover Cluster, we will need to have additional SQL Server Cluster names and IP addresses.

Network name

These are the names by which the environment identifies the SQL Server Cluster (in the earlier version, Virtual SQL Server Name), Windows Server Cluster name, and MSDTC name, among others.

It may happen that we see the network binding warning coming up. In this scenario, we will have to go to **Network and Sharing Center | Change Adapter Settings**. Once there, pressing *Alt + F*, we will select **Advanced Settings**. Select **Public Network** and move it up if it is not and repeat this process on the second node.

Shared disks

In the setup operation I have performed, I have used StarWind iSCSI Software to create the following three virtual shared disks (alternatively, we can use Cluster Shared Volumes):

- One to use for Witness Disks (Quorum)
- One for MSDTC and for SQL Server System Database
- The last for SQL Server User Databases

Please note that if we decide to install file stream, we may want to procure a separate disk for the file share.

Previously, we used to store the unstructured data, such as text, images, videos, and so on, outside the SQL Server database. It was not an easy task when it came to managing them and rebuilding the database server. With the newly introduced FILESTREAM feature, it has become much easier to store and manage the unstructured data within the SQL Server. For more information on FILESTREAM, we can refer to an article at `http://www.simple-talk.com/sql/learn-sql-server/an-introduction-to-sql-server-filestream/`, authored by Jacob Sebastian, an SQL Server MVP.

As the I/O-intensive program could hamper the performance of a Witness Disk, which may cause it to fail and can result in an entire cluster failover, if we have a separate disk for MSDTC, we can use it for the other cluster instance as well. Space management and policies are not directly supported by FILESTREAM. Hence, it should be on a separate disk.

There is one more interesting change we may see with Windows Server 2008 R2 and that is when we add the disk to the cluster. We may now add a disk with a capacity of 16 Exabyte, with added support of partitioning using **GUID Partitioning Table (GPT)**; earlier this was limited to 2 TB with MBR partitioning.

Once we have disks ready on our iSCSI storage, go to "iSCSI Initiator" via **Start | Administrator Tool** and add a portal IP address; this will show us the disks available to be used in a cluster.

In case we are installing a Multi-instance Failover Cluster, it is recommended that we procure additional disks — one for Witness Disk, that is, Quorum, and the other for data (we may have one or more data disks according to our requirement).

Refer to `http://www.sql-server-performance.com/articles/clustering/clustering_best_practices_p1.aspx` for SQL Server Cluster best practices.

Installing a Single-instance Failover Cluster

In the earlier section of this chapter, we learned about the prerequisites for installing a failover cluster. Now that we are aware of them, let's get started by installing Single instance, that is, an Active/Passive cluster.

Let me explain the most important aspect here. The term Active/Passive is used here because this configuration is a two-node and Single-instance Failover Cluster. We should actually practice calling it a Single-instance Failover Cluster instead of calling it an Active/Passive failover.

1. Create and add disks that we will be using while we install the failover cluster. We have to launch an **iSCSI Initiator** tool from **Start | Administrator Tool**.

2. We will see the screen shown in the following screenshot. Here we have to add a target name or an IP address so that the available disks are visible to us. To do so, click **Discover Portal** and add the IP address or DNS name of the target—in our case, it's **SQLNode1**.

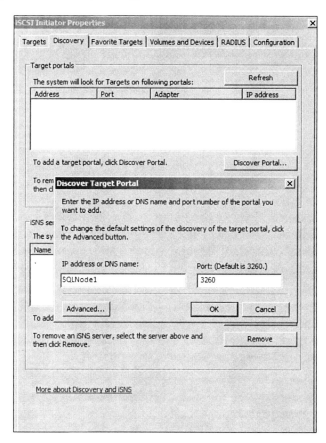

3. Go to the **volumes and devices** section and we will see the list of available disks' images that we can use in our setup. Click on the **Auto Configure** button and all the available disks' statuses will be changed to "Connected" from "inactive".

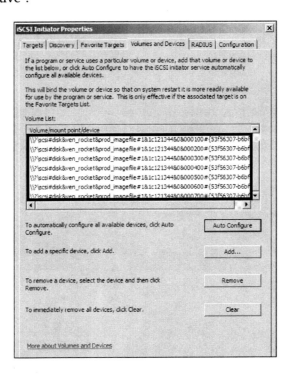

As the disks are added, we can bring them online using the Server Management console or the Disk Management Console (`diskmgmt.mcs`). Once the disks are online, we may initialize and create a partition.

4. Because we will be adding SQL Server as an application on the Windows Cluster server, we should add Application Roles to both the cluster nodes. Open the **Server Manager** console, select **Roles**, and click the **Add Roles** link. From the list of roles, select **Application Server Role**. Under **Application Server Roles**, select **Application Server Foundation**, **Incoming Remote Transaction**, and **Outgoing Remote Transaction**.

5. As we may see in the following screenshot, we have installed the **Application Server** role and also **.Net Framework 3.5.1**, which is a part of the prerequisites.

6. From **Server Console Manager**, select the **Features** tab. From the list of available features, we will have to select **Failover Clustering** so that we can add nodes and form the cluster server to have high availability. Click **Next**.

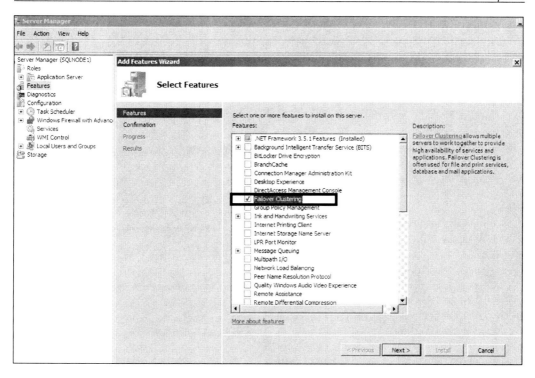

7. Once the installation of failover clustering feature is complete, please verify that the result pane shows a success report.

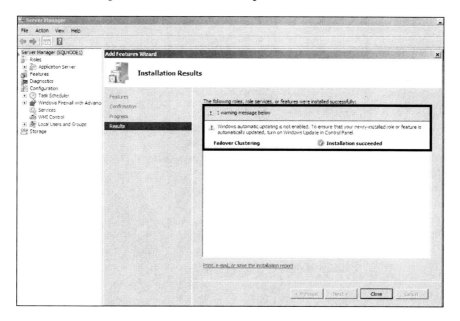

8. Now that we have met all the prerequisites to install cluster, let's validate our cluster nodes to check whether they pass the compatibility tests. Open the **Failover Cluster Manager** from **Start | Administrative tools** and add the Fully Qualified DNS name of the system of both the nodes—in our case, SQLNode1 and SQLNode2.

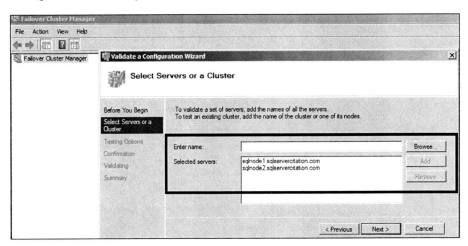

9. Select **Run all tests (recommended)** from the **Testing Options**. This will thoroughly test all the components we made available to build our cluster. If we select the **Run only tests I select** option, it will test selected components, which is not recommended. This is because the component that we have omitted may be the component that's blocking the path and preventing us from being able to install the cluster.

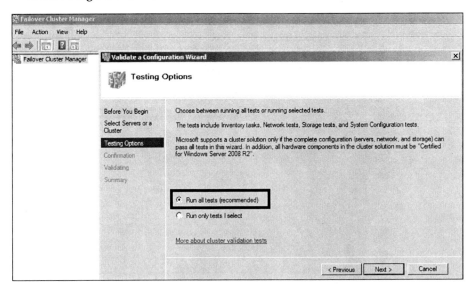

10. After validation finishes, please check the validation report carefully because, based on this, it will be decided whether or not we should continue with the process further. If we see any errors in the validation report, we need to go back and correct them before proceeding further with the installation. This is because failure would cause our installation to stop in the middle or it will not function properly.

In my case, we will see a warning message **Validate All Drivers Signed**. This message comes for the StartWind iSCSI disk drives, which we have used to emulate as iSCSI drives for our configuration here.

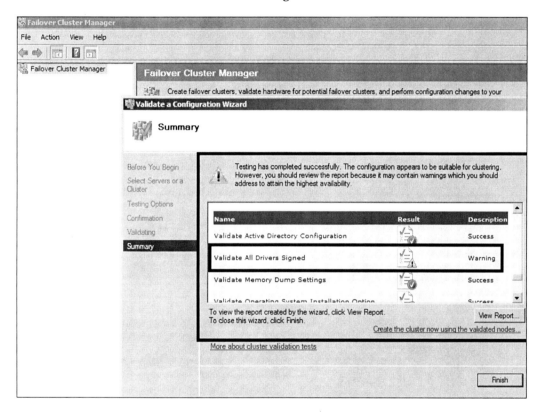

11. As our validation test returns a successful report, we will go ahead and create a Windows Cluster first. From the **Failover Cluster Manager**, select the **Create Cluster** link under the **Management** section.

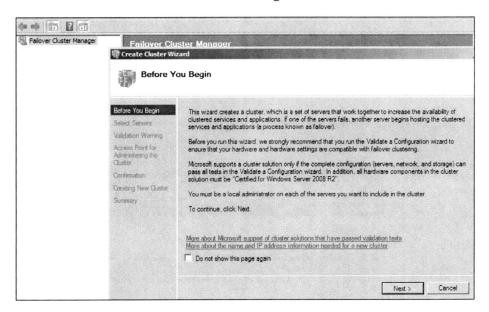

12. Add nodes that we want as part of our cluster—in our case, SQLNode1 and SQLNode2.

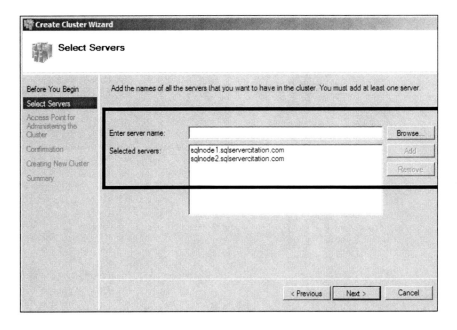

13. In the **Access Point for Administering the Cluster** section, it will ask us to name our cluster server; using this name, we can then manage and administer our Windows Cluster. We will also need to provide an IP address here. Let's give it a name, such as **Win2008Cluster**, and assign an IP address of **192.168.1.5**.

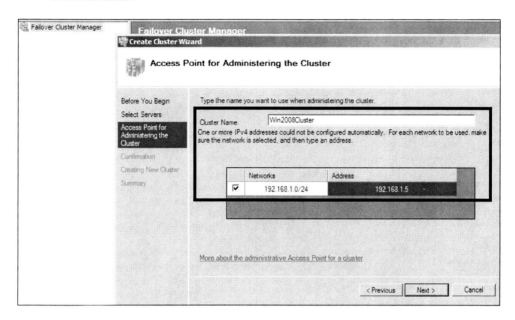

14. At this point, we will see the summary report; please verify that the report returns a successful status.

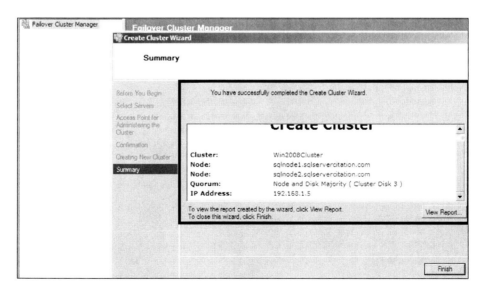

15. As we have finished creating the Windows Cluster, it is a time for us to configure Witness Disk, that is, Quorum, before we proceed further. Although Windows Server 2008 R2 will select the best suitable option to configure Quorum for our cluster, if we want to change this option, we may do so.

Select the cluster that we just created, right-click on it, and select **More Actions… | Configure Cluster Quorum Settings…**.

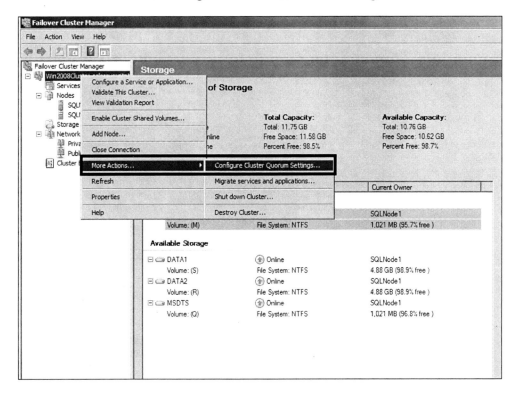

 In the Quorum configuration section, verify that the selected mode is the recommended one.

16. Verify that the disk that is configured as a Witness is the same one we intended to use for Quorum in the **Configure Storage Witness** section. Sometimes wizard uses the first available disk to act as a Quorum and it is not always certain that this was intended to be a Quorum, that is, 100 GB disk.

17. Once we are satisfied with the configuration, click **Finish** and proceed with the next step.

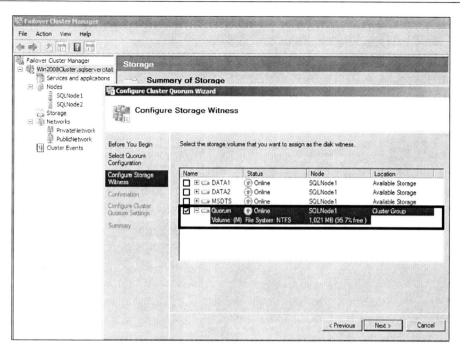

18. Now that we have configured Quorum, we will move on to configuring MSDTC for our cluster. To configure MSDTC, right-click **Services and application** and then select **Select Service or Application | Distributed Transaction Coordinator (DTC)**.

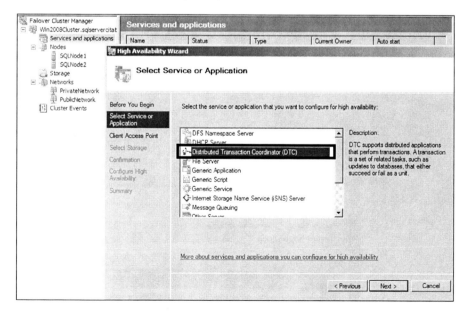

19. On the **Client Access Point** screen, give the name of our MSDTC service and an IP address—in our case, it's **Win2008MSDTS**.

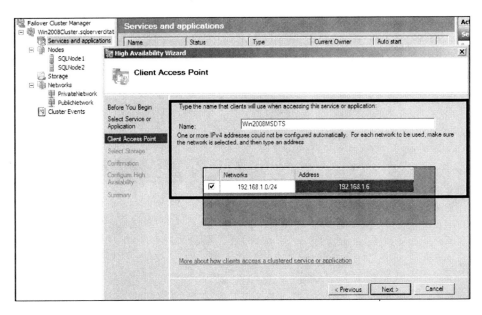

Once we give a name and an IP address, we will have to select the storage we are going to use for MSDTS and confirm it. Please make sure that the report summary returns a successful result.

20. Once we are done, we will be able to see the Win2008MSDTS listed under the **Services and Application** section of the **Failover Cluster Manager** console. We need to click on our MSDTC Service and check if it is online.

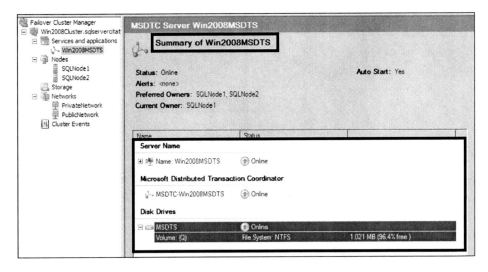

21. At this point, we are all set to go ahead and install SQL Server. Insert the disk and click on `setup.exe`. This will open the **SQL Server Installation Center** screen, as shown in the following screenshot. Click the **New SQL Server Failover Cluster Installation** option under the **Installation** section.

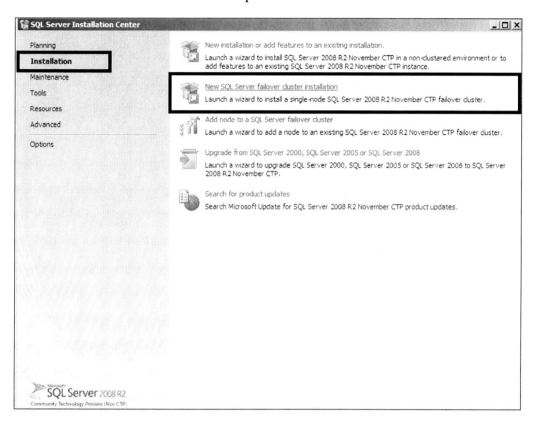

 There are two methods for installing a failover cluster — one is integrated installation with the **Add Node** option and the second is advanced/enterprise installation; we will be using the first option.

22. Here we will have to provide the Key that we had gotten with the installation media. In the next step, we have to accept the license terms and run the setup support file. We have to be a little careful in order to ensure that no error crops up.

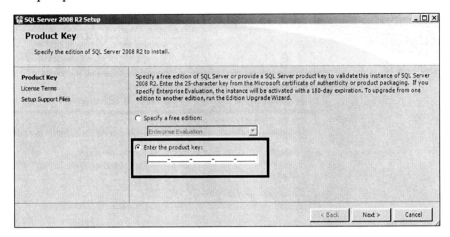

23. In the **Feature Selection** window, select the feature we want to install. The **Shared Feature directory** will be the local disk, whereas the database engine will use another disk—the shared one. Please make sure that the disks where we are installing SQL Server Shared Features have ample space.

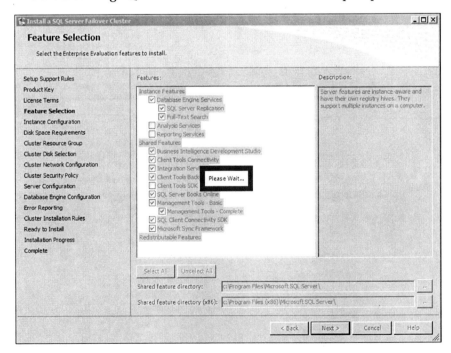

24. In this section, we have to specify the **SQL Server Network Name**. This name is used by the client machines to connect to the SQL Server.

    Generally, the instance name is used as the instance ID; if we want this to be different, we may select the **Instance ID** box and specify the value.

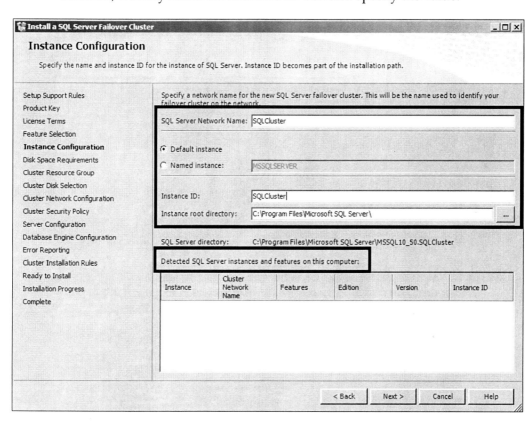

We will notice that there is nothing listed under the **Detected SQL Server Instances and features on this computer** section. This is because we do not have any SQL Server instance running. This section will have some values when we configure a multi-instance cluster in the next section.

25. Please make sure that the disk requirements are met.

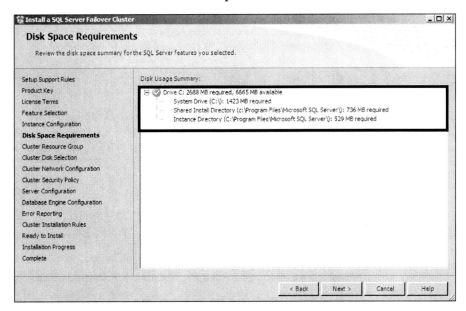

26. In this section, we will have to check if the resources are available on the Windows Cluster. We can use the drop-down box to select any existing resource group or can key-in the name of a new group to create. Click **Next**.

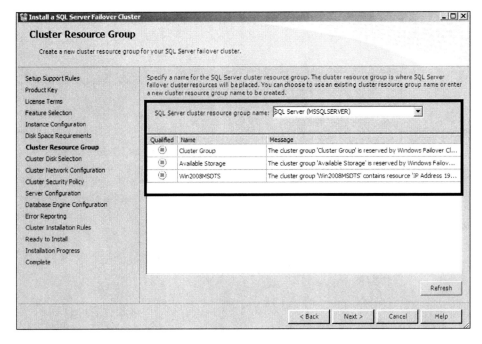

27. In the **Cluster Disk Selection** section, select the available disk(s). This may vary based on the requirement. We have configured four disks earlier for our cluster, and we are going to use both available disks here—one for system databases and the other for user databases.

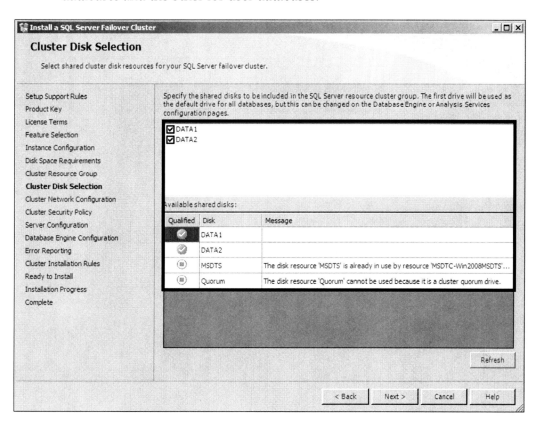

28. The next step is to provide the static IP address under the **Cluster Network Configuration** box.

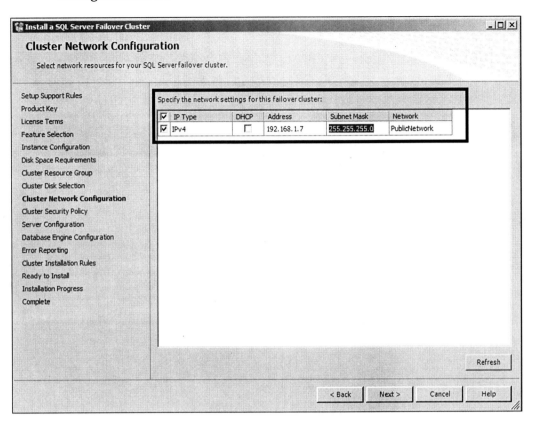

I have disabled the IPv6 protocol because we are not going to use it and this will avoid confusion. In the Cluster Security Policy, we may select the recommended settings (**Use Services SID**), but we have opted to use Domain Group. So, if we are installing SQL Server 2008 on our existing Windows Server 2003, we need not look at some other reference material.

29. As we have opted for Domain Group, we will have to provide the service account credentials for the database engine and for the SQL Server Agent. Select the appropriate collation from the **Collation** tab.

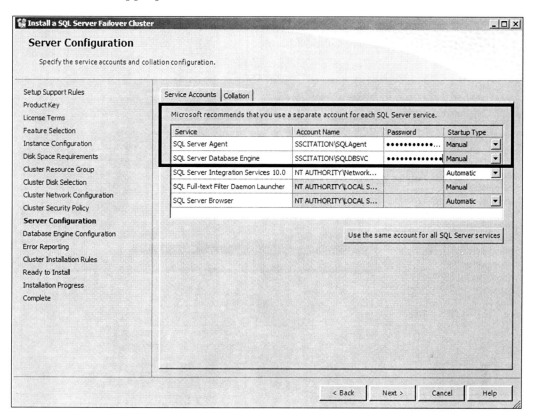

30. In the **Database Engine Configuration** dialog box, select **Mixed Mode** and enter the password. Additionally, if we would like to, we may add the current user as an administrator of the SQL Server that we are installing.

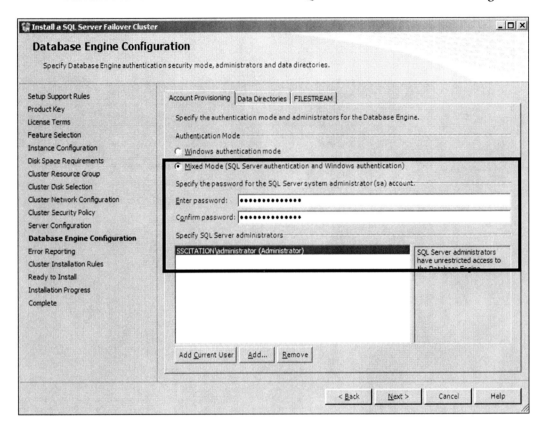

31. In the **Data Directories** tab, we may specify the disk drive based on the requirements. By default, the disk drive mentioned here will be the first shared disk amongst the ones available. If we want to use the FILESTREAM feature, click the **FILESTREAM** tab and configure it in the appropriate way.

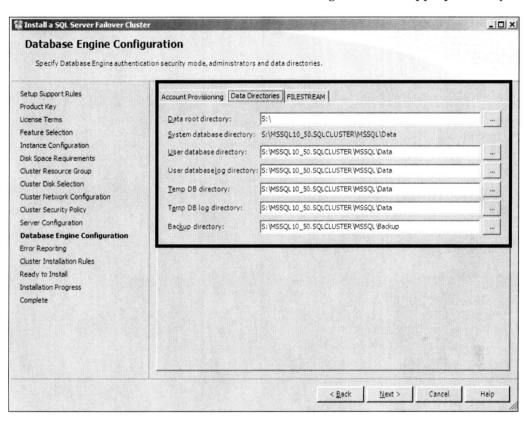

32. In the **Error Reporting** section, click **Next**. In the **Cluster Installation Rules** section, make sure that all checks are successful and click **Next**. In the **Ready to Install** section, verify that the selected features are correctly mentioned and configurations are correct. Clicking **Next** will start the installation.

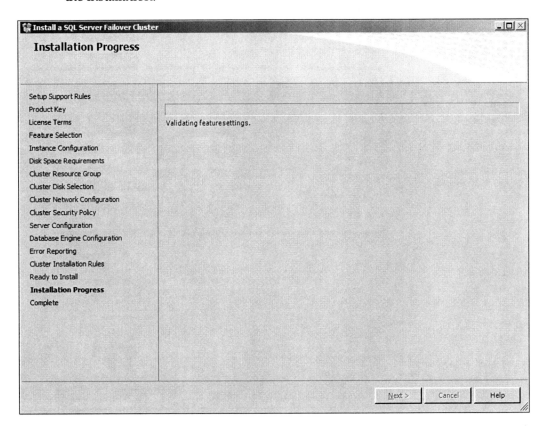

33. The complete dialog box will give us a summary report of whether the installation succeeded or failed, with the reasons if it has failed. Click on the **Close** button to finish the installation.

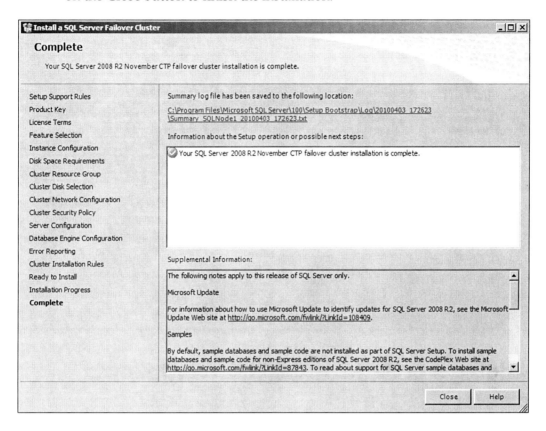

34. By clicking on the SQL Server, we can verify that the SQL Server Cluster is online. Although we have installed SQL Server Cluster and it's up and running, we do not have the high availability as we still have to add a second node.

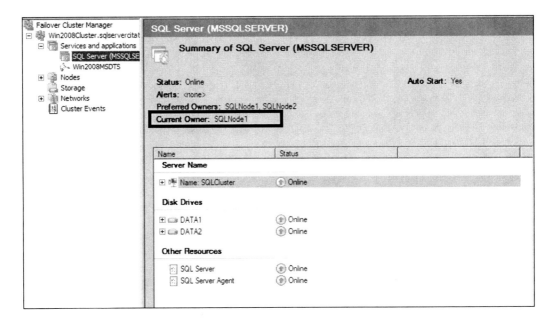

Adding a node to an SQL Server failover cluster

We are done with the cluster installation here, but we still have to add a node to the SQL Server failover cluster so as to make it capable of failover. Let's add a node here.

1. On the second node of the cluster, execute `setup.exe` from the installation media, which will show the **SQL Server Installation Center** screen. From here, we have to select **Add node to a SQL Server Failover Cluster** — in our case, the name of the node is **SQLNode2**.

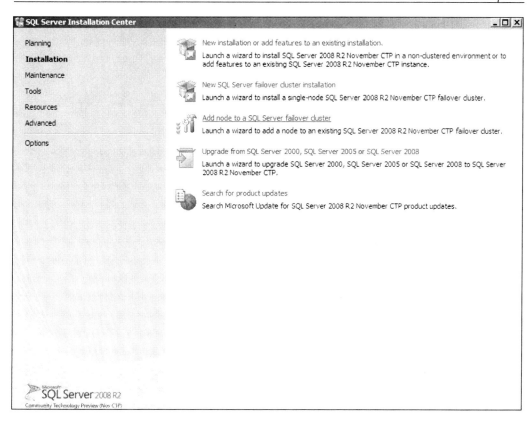

 As most of the screens are similar, we will skip to the add node feature directly.

2. In the **Product Key** dialog box, enter the valid key that comes with the installation media and click **Next**.

3. In the **License** dialog box, accept the license and click **Next**.

4. In the **Setup Support Rules** section, make sure that all the checks are returned as successful and click **Next**.

5   On the **Cluster Node Configuration** screen, verify the **Instance Name**, **Cluster Network Name**, and the features we had installed earlier.

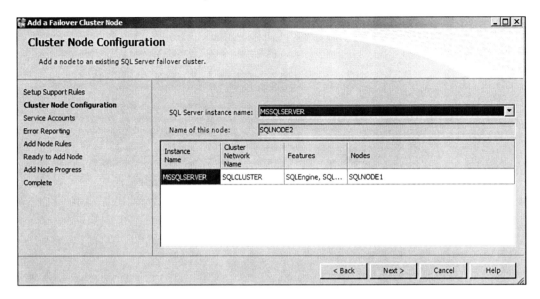

6.   In the **Service Accounts** screen, pass on the credential for the **SQL Server Database Engine** and for the **SQL Server Agent**, and then click **Next**.

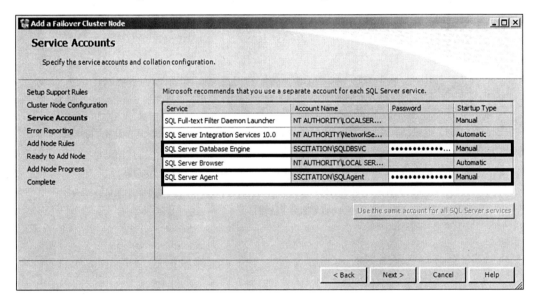

7. In the **Error Reporting** dialog box, click **Next**.

8. In the **Add Node Rules** section, verify that there is no error reported and click **Next**.

9. In the **Ready to add Node**, check that all the all configurations are proper and click **Next**.

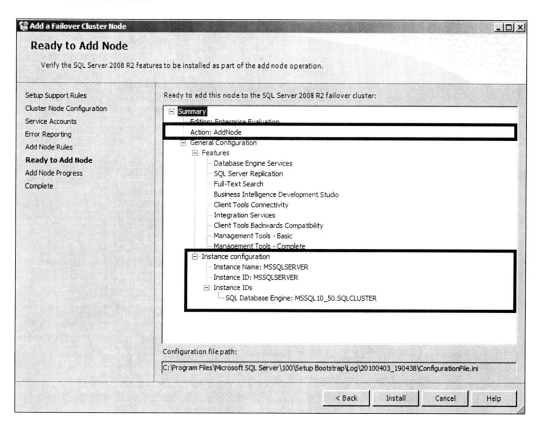

10. The complete dialog box should return a successful report, which concludes a successful installation of the SQL Server 2008 R2 Failover Cluster on the Windows Server 2008 R2.

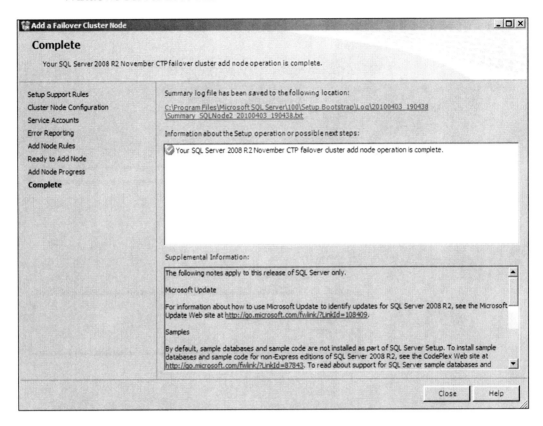

11. We have added a node to the SQL Server failover cluster and we are now ready to test the failover. Open Cluster Administration, right-click on the SQL Server, and select **Move this Service** or **Application to another Node | Move to node SQLNode2**.

After failover to **SQLNode2**, we can see (from the following screenshot) that the current owner is changed to **SQLNode2**:

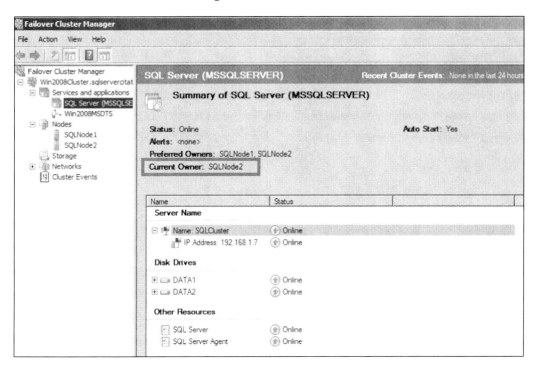

Installing the SQL Server failover cluster using the command prompt

There is another method of installing SQL Server Cluster and that is by using the command prompt. The following is the code:

```
setup.exe /q /ACTION=InstallFailoverCluster

/FEATURES=SQL

/INSTANCENAME="SQLCluster"

/INSTANCEID="SQLCluster"

/INSTANCEDIR="C:\Program Files\Microsoft SQL Server" /
INSTALLSHAREDDIR="C:\Program Files\Microsoft SQL Server" /SQLSVCACCOUNT="
SSCitation\sqldbsvc"

/SQLSVCPASSWORD="XYZ12345"

/AGTSVCACCOUNT="SSCitation\sqlagent"

/AGTSVCPASSWORD="XYZ12345"
```

```
/INSTALLSQLDATADIR= "R:\MSSQLSERVER" /SQLCOLLATION="SQL_Latin1_General_
CP1_CS_AS" /FAILOVERCLUSTERGROUP="MSSQLServer"

/FAILOVERCLUSTERDISKS="disk1" /FAILOVERCLUSTERIPADDRESSES="IPv4;192.168.1
.5;SQLCluster;255.255.255.0"

/FAILOVERCLUSTERNETWORKNAME="SQLCluster" /SQLSYSADMINACCOUNTS="SSCitation
\Administrator"

/SECURITYMODE=SQL

/SAPWD="XYZ12345"

/INSTALLSHAREDWOWDIR="C:\Program Files\Microsoft SQL Server"

/IACCEPTSQLSERVERLICENSETERMS=yes
```

Code for Adding Node:

```
setup.exe /q /ACTION=AddNode /INSTANCENAME="SQLCluster" /SQLSVCACCOUNT="S
SCitation\sqldbsvc" /SQLSVCPASSWORD="XYZ12345" /AGTSVCACCOUNT="SSCitation
\sqlagt" /AGTSVCPASSWORD="XYZ12345"

/IACCEPTSQLSERVERLICENSETERMS=yes
```

The following table shows the explanation for the parameters used in the setup:

Parameter	Explanation
/q	Unattended installation, no user interface
FEATURE	We may need to mention the feature that we may want to install
INSTANCENAME	This is the name of the instance; generally, this is the same as the Instance ID
INSTANCEID	The name of the SQL Server, directory structure, registry, and service name will reflect the instance ID
INSTANCEDIR	Here we will have to specify the root directory path
INSTALLSHAREDDIR	Path for the root of the shared installation
SQLSVCACCOUNT	SQL Server Service Account
SQLSVCPASSWORD	SQL Server Service Account Password
AGTSVCACCOUNT	SQL Server Agent Account
AGTSVCPASSWORD	SQL Server Agent Account Password
INSTALLSQLDATADIR	Root for the Database Engine data
SQLCOLLATION	Collation name for the SQL Server
FAILOVERCLUSTERGROUP	Name of the resource group for SQL Server
FAILOVERCLUSTERDISKS	Associated Disk with SQL Server failover cluster

Parameter	Explanation
FAILOVERCLUSTERIPADDRESSES	IP Type (IPv4 or IPv6), IP Address, Network Name, and Subnet masks; DHCP is also supported
FAILOVERCLUSTERNETWORKNAME	This is the SQL Server Cluster Network name that is used by clients to connect to SQL Server Services
SQLSYSADMINACCOUNTS	Windows Account as a SQL Server System Administrator
SECRITYMODE	Here we will have to specify the Authentication mode; "SQL" is mixed authentication mode
SAPWD	Password for SA
INSTALLSHAREDWODIR	Root installation path for X86-shared feature
IACCEPTSQLSERVERLICENSETERMS	Value should be set to YES

Installing SQL Server failover cluster using the Configuration file

There is another method that we may use to carry out the installation of SQL Server failover cluster through the integrated setup, that is, by using the Configuration file.

The Configuration file will be generated automatically whenever we use the setup wizard. The file is available by the name `configuration.ini` at the following location: on`<drive>:\Program Files\Microsoft SQL Server\100\Setup Bootstrap\Log\<YYYYMMDD_HHMMSS\` directory.

To generate the `Configuraton.ini` file, we have to start the wizard and cancel it before the completion of the **Ready to Install** dialog box. The `Configuration.ini` file contains various parameters and values that we select during the setup. The file won't contain passwords, which means we have to mention passwords manually for security purposes. Another parameter that we have to add manually is `FAILOVERCLUSTERIPADDRESSES` and mention its value. We can use this configuration file for unattended installations. The following is the code that we can see in the `Configuration.ini` file:

```
;SQLSERVER2008 Configuration File
[SQLSERVER2008]

; Specify the Instance ID for the SQL Server features you have
specified. SQL Server directory structure, registry structure, and
service names will reflect the instance ID of the SQL Server instance.
INSTANCEID="SQLCluster"
```

```
; Specifies a Setup work flow, like INSTALL, UNINSTALL, or UPGRADE.
This is a required parameter.
ACTION="InstallFailoverCluster"
; Specifies features to install, uninstall, or upgrade. The list of
top-level features include SQL, AS, RS, IS, and Tools. The SQL feature
will install the database engine, replication, and full-text. The
Tools feature will install Management Tools, Books online, Business
Intelligence Development Studio, and other shared components.
FEATURES=SQLENGINE,REPLICATION,FULLTEXT,BIDS,CONN,IS,BC,BOL,SSMS,ADV_
SSMS,SNAC_SDK,OCS
; Displays the command line parameters usage
HELP="False"
; Specifies that the detailed Setup log should be piped to the
console.
INDICATEPROGRESS="False"
; Setup will not display any user interface.
QUIET="False"
; Setup will display progress only without any user interaction.
QUIETSIMPLE="False"
; Specifies that Setup should install into WOW64. This command line
argument is not supported on an IA64 or a 32-bit system.
X86="False"
; Detailed help for command line argument ENU has not been defined
yet.
ENU="True"
; Parameter that controls the user interface behavior. Valid values
are Normal for the full UI, and AutoAdvance for a simplified UI.
UIMODE="Normal"
; Specify if errors can be reported to Microsoft to improve future SQL
Server releases. Specify 1 or True to enable and 0 or False to disable
this feature.
ERRORREPORTING="False"
; Specify the root installation directory for native shared
components.
INSTALLSHAREDDIR="c:\Program Files\Microsoft SQL Server"
; Specify the root installation directory for the WOW64 shared
components.
INSTALLSHAREDWOWDIR="c:\Program Files (x86)\Microsoft SQL Server"
; Specify the installation directory.
INSTANCEDIR="C:\Program Files\Microsoft SQL Server"
; Specify that SQL Server feature usage data can be collected and sent
to Microsoft. Specify 1 or True to enable and 0 or False to disable
this feature.
SQMREPORTING="False"
; Specify a default or named instance. MSSQLSERVER is the default
instance for non-Express editions and SQLExpress for Express editions.
```

This parameter is required when installing the SQL Server Database
Engine (SQL), Analysis Services (AS), or Reporting Services (RS).
INSTANCENAME="MSSQLSERVER"
; Specifies a cluster shared disk to associate with the SQL Server
failover cluster instance.
FAILOVERCLUSTERDISKS="DATA1" "DATA2"
; Specifies the name of the cluster group for the SQL Server failover
cluster instance.
FAILOVERCLUSTERGROUP="SQL Server (MSSQLSERVER)"
; Specifies the name of the SQL Server failover cluster instance.
This name is the network name that is used to connect to SQL Server
services.
FAILOVERCLUSTERNETWORKNAME="SQLCluster"
; Agent account name
AGTSVCACCOUNT="SSCITATION\SQLAgent"
; Startup type for Integration Services.
ISSVCSTARTUPTYPE="Automatic"
; Account for Integration Services: Domain\User or system account.
ISSVCACCOUNT="NT AUTHORITY\NetworkService"
; Controls the service startup type setting after the service has been
created.
ASSVCSTARTUPTYPE="Automatic"
; The collation to be used by Analysis Services.
ASCOLLATION="Latin1_General_CI_AS"
; The location for the Analysis Services data files.
ASDATADIR="Data"
; The location for the Analysis Services log files.
ASLOGDIR="Log"
; The location for the Analysis Services backup files.
ASBACKUPDIR="Backup"
; The location for the Analysis Services temporary files.
ASTEMPDIR="Temp"
; The location for the Analysis Services configuration files.
ASCONFIGDIR="Config"
; Specifies whether or not the MSOLAP provider is allowed to run in
process.
ASPROVIDERMSOLAP="1"
; A port number used to connect to the SharePoint Central
Administration web application.
FARMADMINPORT="0"
; Level to enable FILESTREAM feature at (0, 1, 2 or 3).
FILESTREAMLEVEL="0"
; Specifies a Windows collation or an SQL collation to use for the
Database Engine.
SQLCOLLATION="SQL_Latin1_General_CP1_CI_AS"

```
; Account for SQL Server service: Domain\User or system account.
SQLSVCACCOUNT="SSCITATION\SQLDBSVC"
; Windows account(s) to provision as SQL Server system administrators.
SQLSYSADMINACCOUNTS="SSCITATION\administrator"
; The default is Windows Authentication. Use "SQL" for Mixed Mode
Authentication.
SECURITYMODE="SQL"
; The Database Engine root data directory.
INSTALLSQLDATADIR="S:"
; Specifies how the startup mode of the report server NT service. When
; Manual - Service startup is manual mode (default).
; Automatic - Service startup is automatic mode.
; Disabled - Service is disabled
RSSVCSTARTUPTYPE="Automatic"
; Specifies which mode report server is installed in.
; Default value: "FilesOnly"
RSINSTALLMODE="FilesOnlyMode"
; Add description of input argument FTSVCACCOUNT
FTSVCACCOUNT="NT AUTHORITY\LOCAL SERVICE"


"
```

Now, we have to execute the following command from the command prompt to initiate the setup process:

```
Setup.exe /q /Configurationfile="C:\SQLSetup\ConfigurationFile.ini
```

As we have installed the SQL Server failover cluster, we shall be adding a node using the `Configuration.ini` file, which has the following parameter.

SQLSERVER2008 Configuration File:

```
[SQLSERVER2008]

ACTION=AddNode
INSTANCENAME="SQLCluster"
SQLSVCACCOUNT="SSCitation\SQLDBSVC"
SQLSVCPASSWORD="XYZ12345"
AGTSVCACCOUNT="SSCitation\SQLAGTSVC"
AGTSVCPASSWORD="XYZ12345"
```

Once we have the `configuration.ini` file ready for use, execute the following command from the command prompt on Node2—in our case, SQLNode2.

```
Setup.exe /q /Configurationfile="C:\SQLAddNode\ConfigurationFile.ini
```

If we opt to remove the cluster for any reason, it can be done using the `configuration.ini` file, which contains the following code:

```
;SQLSERVER2008 Configuration File
[SQLSERVER2008]

ACTION="RemoveNode"
INSTANCENAME="SQLCluster"
FAILOVERCLUSTERNETWORKNAME="SQLCluster"
```

Execute the following command to initiate the removal of the cluster node.

```
Setup.exe /q /Configurationfile="C:\RemoveNode\ConfigurationFile.ini"
```

Installing Multi-instance (Active/Active) Failover Cluster

We have just covered the installation procedure for the Single-instance Failover Cluster for SQL Server 2008 R2. Now let's move on and have a look at Multi-instance, that is, the Active/Active Failover Cluster. Before we get started, I would like to clear some queries.

- **Query**: What is the difference between Active/Passive and Active/Active Failover Cluster?

  Answer: In reality, there is only one difference between Single-instance (Active/Passive Failover Cluster) and Multi-instance (Active/Active Failover Cluster). As its name suggests, in a Multi-instance cluster, there will be two or more SQL Server active instances running in a cluster, compared to one instance running in Single-instance. Also, to configure a multi-instance Cluster, we may need to procure additional disks, IP addresses, and network names for the SQL Server.

- **Query**: What is the benefit of having Multi-instance, that is, Active/Active configuration?

  Answer: Depending on the business requirement and the capability of our hardware, we may have one or more instances running in our cluster environment.

  The main goal is to have a better uptime and better High Availability by having multiple SQL Server instances running in an environment. Should anything go wrong with the one SQL Server instance, another instance can easily take over the control and keep the business-critical application up and running!

- **Query**: What is the main purpose of Multi-instance, that is, Active/Active Failover Cluster—load balancing or performance boosting?

  Answer: Technically no. SQL Server failover clustering is for High Availability only. But with multiple instances, we can have two separate applications pointing to separate instances and can redirect the traffic and hence can increase performance. This is how we can balance the network traffic.

- **Query**: What will be the difference in the prerequisites for the Multi-instance Failover Cluster as compared to the Single-instance Failover Cluster?

  Answer: There will be no difference compared to a Single-instance Failover Cluster, except that we need to procure additional disk(s), network name, and IP addresses. We need to make sure that our hardware is capable of handling requests that come from client machines for both the instances.

Installing a Multi-instance cluster is almost similar to adding a Single-instance cluster, except for the need to add a few resources along with a couple of steps here and there. So, while explaining the setup, I will skip some common screenshots.

1. As I said earlier, we will need to procure additional disks so that we can keep our data on it. So, let's arrange additional disk resources for the Multi-instance Failover Cluster.

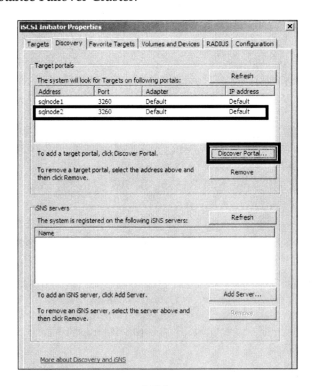

Go to **Start | Administrative Tools | iSCSI Initiator** and click **Discover Portal** under the target panel, as shown in the preceding screenshot. Here, we will provide the name of the target system on which we have procured additional disk resources for our cluster—in our case, SQLNode2.

2. Select the **Target** tab and we will be able to see that some resources are available but they are **Inactive**.

3. Select any of the devices and click **Connect**. This will open the following screen. Click **OK** to make the device **Connected**.

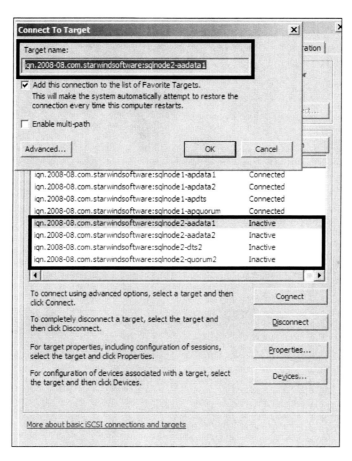

4. Select the **Volumes and Devices** tab. We will see the only four volumes; the one that we added in step 2 is still not available here.

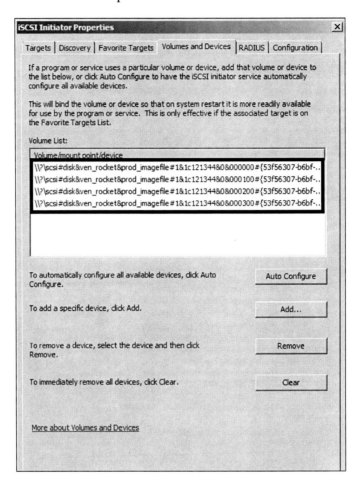

5. Click **Auto Configure** and this will list the recently added devices.

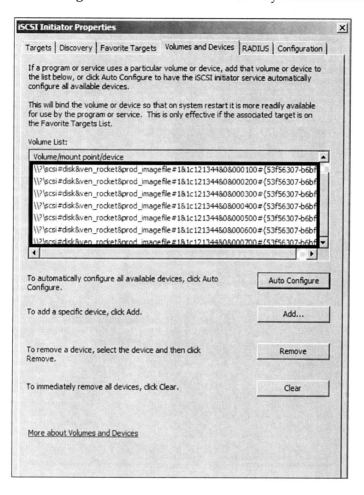

6. Come back to the **Favorite Targets** tab and we will see the name of all the devices that are available for use in the cluster.

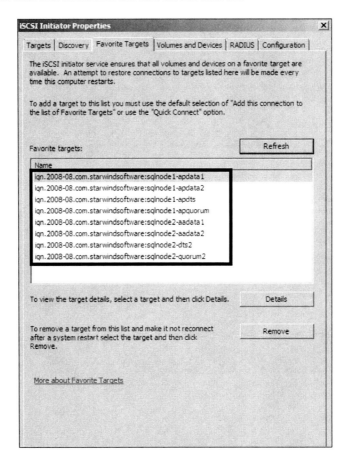

7. At this point, we are all set to go ahead and install SQL Server. Insert the disk and click `setup.exe`. This will bring us the **SQL Server Installation Center** screen. Select the **New SQL Server Failover Cluster Installation** under the **Installation** section.

8. Here we will have to provide the key that we received with the installation media. In the next step, we have to accept the license terms and run the setup support files; here we have to be a little careful when making sure that no error comes up.

9. In the feature selection window, select the feature we want to install. The **Shared Feature directory** will be the local disk, whereas Database Engine will use another disk—the shared one. Please make sure that the disks where we are installing the SQL Server Shared Features have ample space.

10. There can only be one default instance per node, and to avoid confusion, we will have a named instance this time, say SQL2008Inst1. We will keep the same name for the network name of the SQL Server, **Named Instance**, and **Instance ID** just to avoid confusion.

We can also notice that in the following screenshot, there is an entry in the **Detected SQL Server Instances and Features on this Computer** section. This entry shows the name of the SQL Server Failover instance we have created in the *Installing Single-instance Failover Cluster* section.

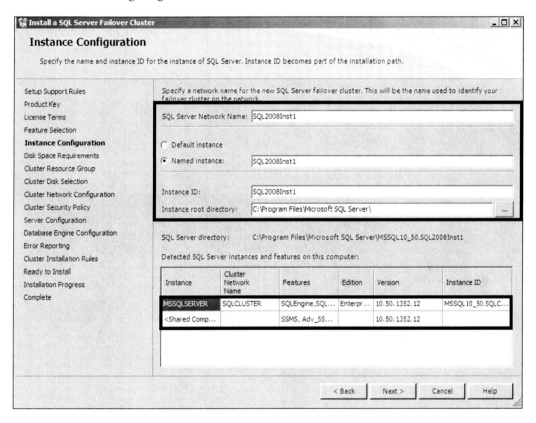

11. In the **Disk Space Requirements** section, verify that we have ample space to install a second instance.

12. In the **Cluster Disk Selection** dialog box, we will select the disk that we
    have added and will keep the same resource group or we can type the new
    resource group in the drop-down box to create a new resource group.

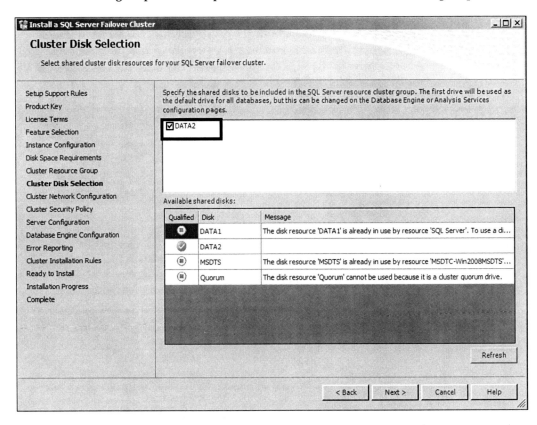

13. In the **Cluster Network Configuration** dialog box, provide the new IP address.

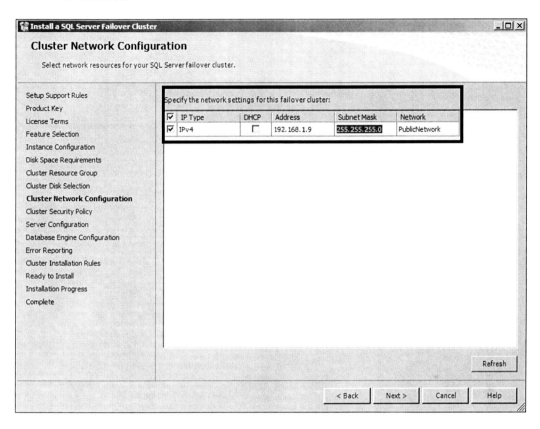

14. In the **Cluster Security Policy** section, we will keep the recommended setting—**Use services SIDs**.

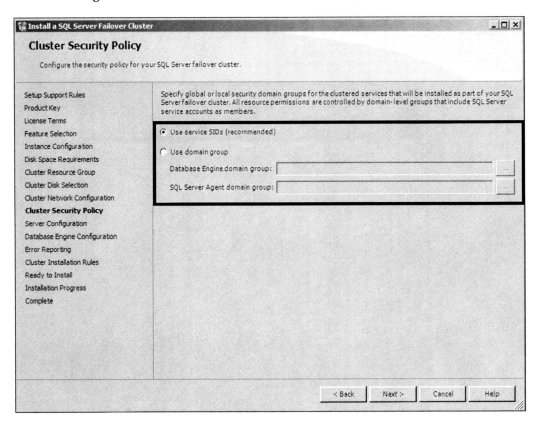

15. In the **Server Configuration** dialog, provide the credentials.

16. In the **Database Engine Configuration** section, select **Mixed Mode** and provide a strong password for the SQL Server System Administrator a.k.a. SA account. If we wish, we may add the current user as a SQL Server Administrator by clicking **Add Current User**.

17. In the **Database Engine Configuration** dialog box, we will see the drive letter for the disk that we have selected in the Cluster Disk Selection. If we wish to use the FILESTREAM feature, you may do so by clicking on the **FILESTREAM** tab and providing the appropriate configuration.

18. In the **Error Reporting** dialog box, click **Next**.

19. Please check and verify that the cluster installation rule doesn't have any errors.

20. In the **Ready to Install** dialog, verify that the configuration is what we intend to install for the new instance.

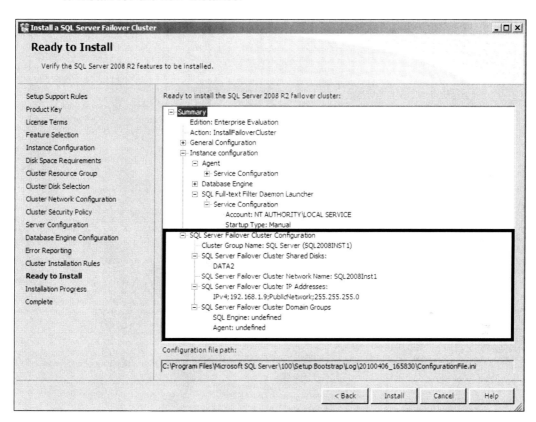

21. In the **Complete** dialog box, please verify that there is no error reported. If the box shows the installation is successful, it is an indication that we have successfully installed a named instance of SQL Server failover cluster.

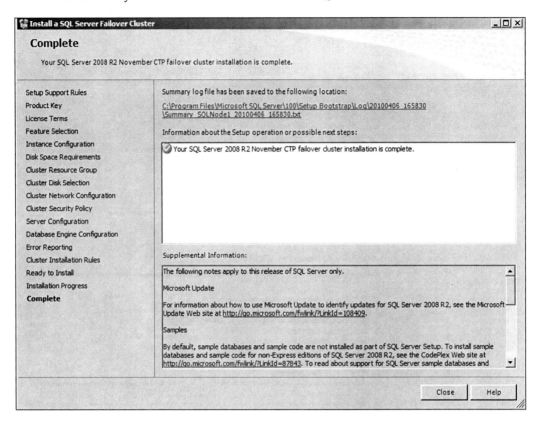

22. Refer to the following screenshot. There are two SQL Server instances listed—one is the default instance that we have installed in the previous section and the newly installed named instance SQL2008Ins1.

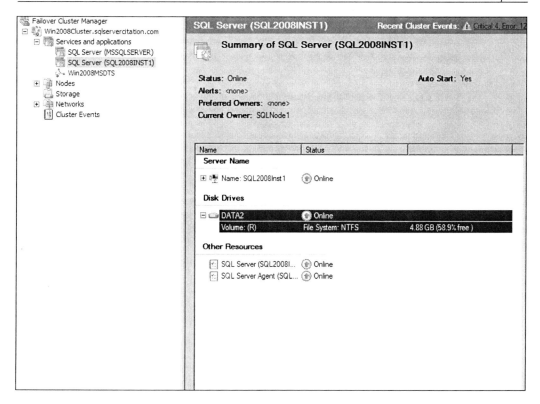

Adding a node to a SQL Server failover cluster

We are done with the installation of a cluster, but this is not the complete setup; we still have to add a node so as to make it a failover cluster. So, let's add a node here:

1. Execute `setup.exe` from the installation media on the second node and select **Installation** from the menu on the left side. On the right-hand side of screen, select **Add node to a SQL Server Failover Cluster**.

2. In the **Setup Support Rules** dialog box, verify that it reports a successful result.

3. In the **Product Key dialog** box, provide the product key supplied with the installation media.

4. Accept the license terms and click **Next**.

5. In the **Cluster Node Configuration** dialog box, we will find the name of the instance for which we have to add another. In our case, **SQL2008Ins1** is the instance name and **SQLNode2** will be the node that we are going to add to the existing cluster.

    We will also see the default installed instance that we had installed previously and the nodes for the instance—**SQLNode1** and **SQLNode2**.

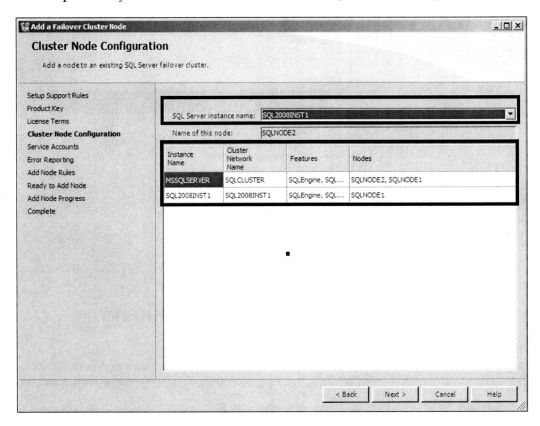

6. In the **Service Accounts** dialog box, enter the credential for the SQL Server and Agent Services accounts.

7. In the **Error Reporting** dialog box, click **Next**.

8. In the **Add Node Rules** dialog, verify that it returns the successful report.

9. In the **Ready to Add Node** dialog box, confirm that the configurations are the same as what we had selected and click **Install**.

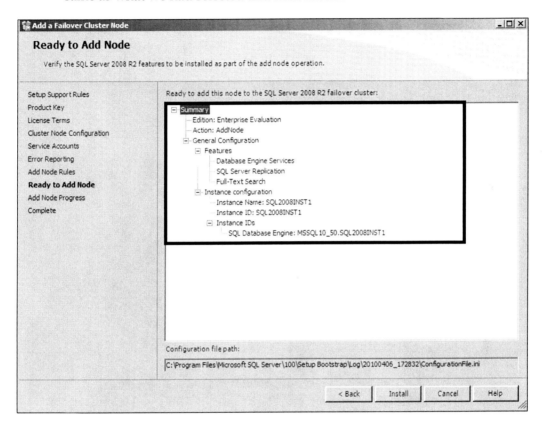

10. Please verify that the **Complete** dialog box doesn't have any error reported.

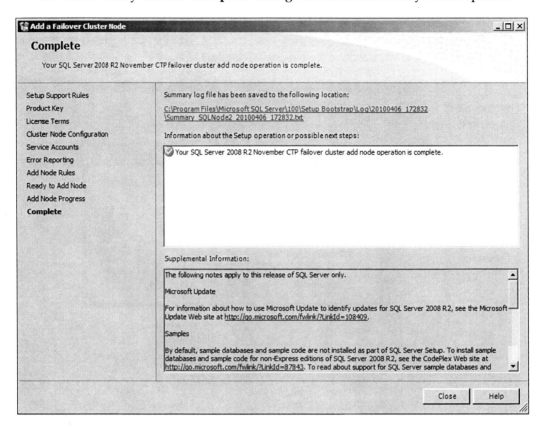

Thus we have installed the second instance of the SQL Server failover cluster.

11. In the **Failover Cluster Manager** console, click on the name of the second instance and we will see the name of the current owner—**SQLNode2** in our case.

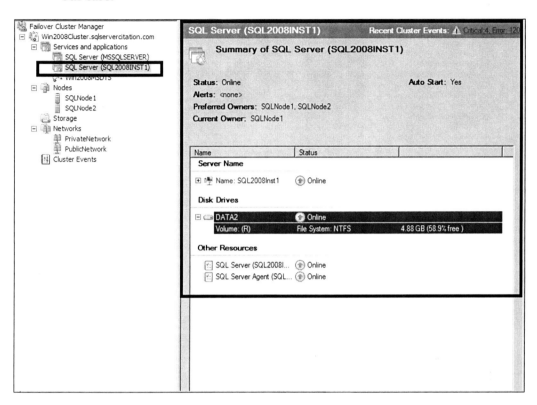

12. At this point, we have a two-nodes Multi-instance SQL Server failover cluster installed. Let's test it by failing it to SQLNode2.

13. Refer to the following screenshot. We will notice that there are two SQL Server failover clusters installed—one is the default instance (**MSSQLServer**) and the second is named instance (**SQL2008Ins1**). The default instance is owned by **SQLNode1** and the named instance is owned by **SQLNode2**.

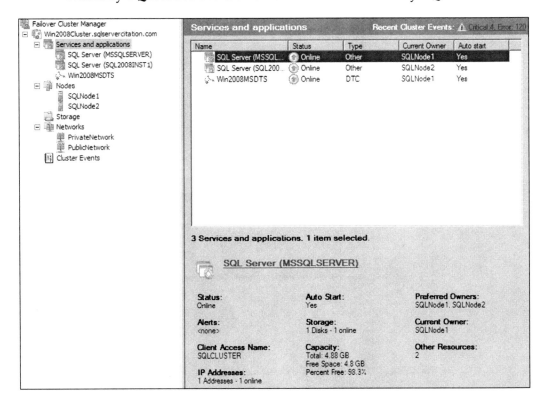

Configuration

In the previous chapter, we learned what clustering is, what are the different types of clustering available, and how they work. We also learned about the different components of SQL Server clusters such as Quorum. We learned how to install Single-instance and Multi-instance SQL Server failover clusters.

In this section, we will learn how to configure SQL Server failover cluster, so that it will give us a boost in performance.

Write caching

If we are using a non-external disk controller with our cluster, we should turn off the write caching as it may hinder performance. This is because data resides in a local disk and there is no guarantee that the data will be available if the disk fails and so there are chances of data loss during failover. However, external controllers can cache correctly.

File shares

We should not use the same drive that is being used as clustered disk, for file share, to prevent failover of cluster group and to have less impact in recovery time if anything goes wrong.

Maximum memory size

It is recommended that we set the maximum memory to about 80 to 90 percent of the total memory (reserved memory for OS+ other applications/number of SQL Server instances). After allocating the maximum memory, we should monitor the statistics for analysis and to optimize it further.

Minimum memory size

We should set the minimum memory in two cases:

- When we have configured maximum memory
- When there are multiple SQL Server instances

This will help reduce the failover time.

Preferred owners

This term is used for nodes that can be the owner of the SQL Server. In case failover occurs, this property will then decide which node is a candidate to own the resources and can take over the control to handle user connection and to run SQL Server services.

This is useful, especially when we have to evict the node from the cluster and then rejoin it to be part of the failover cluster.

LooksAlive

In the previous chapter, we learned what LooksAlive is. Though we can change the default value for the LooksAlive interval, which is set to five seconds, it is recommended to keep it intact.

IsAlive

IsAlive is a thorough health check, which executes every 60 seconds by default. Again, we can change the settings here, though it is recommended that we leave it as it is.

Restart

For most of the resources, we should keep this option selected as we will always want every cluster resource to be available and online.

Affect the Group

This is an important option and should be turned on for the resources that have cluster-wide impact on failover. In this case, it should be immediate failover—usually for SQL Server Engine Server.

We should not select this property for the **SQL Server Agent Service**, **MSDTC**, **BackupDrives**, and **FileSharefolders**.

Dependencies

This property is configurable and requires a lot of attention. This is because if we commit a mistake while configuring this property, it will result in a false alarm some times, so we have to be very careful while we configure the dependencies. We should set SQL Server Agent's dependency on SQL Server Engine Services.

File share

We can configure replication or log shipping with the Failover Clustering. Consider a situation wherein we have configured Transaction Replication for the mission-critical database and the folder that contains the shared data is on the local disk. In some unpleasant moment of failover, this folder won't be available to another node that has taken over the control and it is therefore a good idea to have the shared disk as a resource.

For further information on how to create file share on a cluster, refer to the Microsoft KB article at http://support.microsoft.com/kb/224967.

Anti Virus tool

It is recommended to not install any Anti Virus (AV) tool on the database server. However, if the Information Security Officer insists on installing an AV tool, we should exclude the SQL Server data files (.mdf, .ldf, and .ndf) and SQL Server backup files (.bak and .trn).

 We can refer to the http://support.microsoft.com/kb/309422 site to read about the guidelines for choosing the antivirus software.

Summary

In this chapter, we learned how to set up a Multi-Instance (Active/Active) SQL Server failover cluster and mainly what is the difference between a Single-instance and a Multi-instance SQL Server failover cluster. We also learned what are the advantages of the Multi-Instance SQL Server failover cluster over the Single-instance Failover Cluster.

Snapshot Replication

3

Some time ago, Mr. Young contacted Mr. Old to ask for his advice on what could be the best possible solution to his requirements. Mr. Young works in a large manufacturing company, XY Incorporation, where they have two production boxes, one for developing and the other for testing. They keep only database backup files as the source of recovery in case of any emergency. Now, Mr. Young's boss wanted him to redesign the system architecture so that they don't have to rely on the database backup files for data recovery. The boss also wanted faster report generation. The boss told Mr. Young that would be fine if the reports show data that are few hours old or a day old, but this should be settled in such a way that the company shouldn't have to invest in getting new hardware. After discussing the task at hand with Mr. Old, Mr. Young realized there are two important requirements for his database server.

- A database server that can be used in the case of an emergency
- A Reporting server that provides point-in-time or near real-time reports

Keeping in mind the requirements realized by Mr. Young, we can advise him to go for the Snapshot Replication so as to fulfill both his requirements. Let's now learn about replication in general and its different subtypes.

Snapshot Replication replicates the data/database to one or more than one location. Replication was first introduced in SQL Server 6 with minor support, and was later enhanced in SQL Server 7.0. With the launch of SQL Server 2000, some additional features have been added to it. With SQL Server 2005, Microsoft has introduced Peer-to-Peer Replication, which has the capability of load balancing.

Configuration Replication purely depends on the business requirement, that is, for the purpose of reporting:

- Data from more than one location needs to be merged to a central location
- Data from more than one location is stored to a central location
- We may want to have load balancing with the replication

Microsoft SQL Server supports four different types of replication, including one subtype.

- Snapshot Replication
- Merge Replication
- Transactional Replication
- Peer-to-Peer Replication

Before we dive into details, let's first walk through the definition and have a look at the components of each type.

Components of the replication

Before we start, let's have an overview of the different components of replication.

- **Publisher**: It is a server that publishes the data. This server hosts the database that will act as the source of the data to be published.

- **Distributor**: It is a server that is responsible for distributing data to the Subscriber(s).

- **Subscribers**: These are the servers that have the subscription database. The Distributor sends the data to the Subscriber server. The data is then published by the Publisher. The Subscriber can be configured either by using the Pull or Push method.

- **Push Subscription**: In this method of subscribing data, Agent connects to the Subscriber periodically and **pushes the data** that is marked for replication to the Subscriber. Hence, the subscription is referred to as Push Subscription.

- **Pull Subscription**: In this method of subscribing data, Agent connects to the Distribution Database periodically and **pulls the data** marked for replication. Therefore, this subscription is referred to as Pull Subscription.

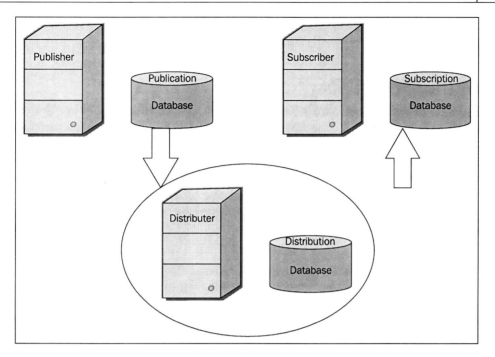

Types of replication

There are three types of replication available. **Snapshot Replication** is the simplest and is unidirectional replication. **Transactional Replication** is also a unidirectional type of replication that replicates data at the transaction level; this type of replication can be bidirectional if it is configured using updatable subscription. **Peer-to-Peer** type of replication is built on top of Transactional Replication; it is a bidirectional type of replication that provides us with an advantage of load balancing. **Merge Replication** is the most complex and bidirectional type of replication.

Let's have a look at these different types of replication in detail.

Snapshot Replication

Snapshot Replication is the simplest type of replication. As the name implies, it takes a snapshot of the published database, connects to the Subscriber server, and then applies the snapshot on the Subscriber. This is the most suitable type of replication when data is required for the purpose of reporting and is not updated at the Subscriber end, or where high latency is acceptable.

Snapshot replication is applied especially in places where data is used to generate point-in-time reporting or near real-time reporting.

Transactional Replication

In this mode of replication, data is replicated at the transaction level by continuous monitoring. To achieve this, Log Reader Agent is being created when Transactional Replication is configured. In Transactional Replication, every transaction marked for replication is monitored by the Log Reader Agent and copied to the distribution database, and then, based on the configuration of where Distribution agent is running, data is either pulled or pushed. Typically, Transactional Replication doesn't allow data to be modified at the end, if it is not configured with immediate update or Queued updating.

 Transactional Replication with Queued Update and Immediate Update will be deprecated in the coming version of SQL Server.

Transactional Replication is widely applied where higher latency is not allowed, data is used for the purpose of reporting, and sometimes Subscriber is allowed to perform updates. Transactional Replication is also used to make database(s) highly available and can be used for disaster recovery purposes. As the Transactional Replication allows near real-time replication, we can use the database(s) in case of any damage at the Publication's/Publisher's end.

 Latency is purely based on how much latency is allowed in our environment and how big the volume of data is. If the volume of the data is large, it would take a longer time to replicate, which should be kept in mind while designing replication for an environment.

Merge Replication

This is the most complex topology of replication. Merge Replication uses triggers to track the changes, taking place at the row level at the Subscriber's as well as the Publisher's end, and based on the changes recorded, it merges the records to another location, irrespective of whether it is the Subscriber or Publisher who updates/inserts records.

Because updates/modifications are allowed in the Merge Replication from one or more than one Subscriber at a time, it has an in-built facility to resolve conflict. There can be many cases wherein Merge Replication is best suited, including:

- Multiple Subscribers update the same data at various times and propagate those changes to the Publisher and to other Subscribers

- There is a chance of conflict

- One time modification is done at the Subscriber end and the same needs to be updated at the Publisher as well as the other Subscriber end

Peer-to-Peer Replication

This has been introduced with the launch of SQL Server 2005. In Peer-to-Peer Replication, the participants have the complete schema and all the data modifications (DML operations) are made at all nodes.

One might wonder what the catch is here and what is newer than Merge Replication. Well, the simplest answer is Peer-to-Peer Replication is designed for **load balancing** purpose by spreading out write activity across all available nodes, and then, based on the sync latency, it synchronizes the database, making read operations faster. We can also notice the speed in the write operation as the write operation will be carried out by separate heads to write to the physical disks, and for that, it has to reach out to the separate node in the network. Additionally, if any of the servers is not available, it will continue to perform with other nodes and the write operation for this node is routed to another node. Peer-to-Peer Replication is best suited for online shopping applications.

Replication topologies

Mainly, there are three different topologies that are used while designing and implementing replication: Central Publisher, Central Subscriber, and Publishing Subscriber. Let's have a quick look at each of them now.

- **Central Publisher**: This is a very common and general type of design. In this topology, there will be a single Publisher and one or more Subscribers. The Distributor server can be the same machine as the Publisher, but it is recommended to use a different physical server as the Distributor.

- **Central Subscriber**: This type of design is used for reporting or OLAP or BI kind of requirement, when business data needs to be analyzed from a single location, no matter which location it comes from — be it from a physically dispersed location or from more than one Publisher.

- **Publishing Subscriber**: In this scenario, the Subscriber of one or more than one publication acts as a Publisher for one or more than one Subscriber. This scenario is useful when there is a low bandwidth between WAN or VPN.

How replication works

In the diagram under the *Components of the replication* section at the Publisher end, we can see that all the data marked for replication is either pulled or pushed at the Distributor database, which later is pulled at or pushed by at the Subscriber end. Now, all this work has to be done on a continuous or a scheduled interval, based on the company policy. The process of replication creates some agents whose work is to send and receive data. There are different types of replication agents for different types of replications. Let's go through each of them, although we will have detailed information on each of them in a separate chapter.

- **Snapshot Agent**: The Snapshot Agent is typically used with all types of replication. The Snapshot Agent's work is to prepare schema and initial data files of the published tables and other objects like stored procedures. Snapshot Agent runs at the Distributor end.

- **Log Reader Agent**: Log Reader Agent is used with Transactional Replication; it moves all transactions that are marked for replication to the distribution database on the Distributor server from the Publisher server. Every database that is published using Transactional Replication has its own Log Reader Agent that runs on the Distributor.

 The Distribution server can be the same physical server as the Publisher server, although it is recommended that we have a different Publisher and Distributor server.

- **Distribution Agent**: This agent is used with Transactional and Snapshot Replication. The Distribution Agent's work is to apply the initial snapshot to the Subscriber and move every transaction from the distribution database to the Subscriber. There is little difference here though: if we have configured Push subscription, Distributor Agent will run on the Distributor, and if it is configured for Pull subscription, Distributor Agent will run at the Subscriber end.

- **Merge Agent**: This agent is available with Merge Replication. Merge Agent's work is to apply the initial snapshot to the Subscriber and keep track of the changes that occurred at either the Subscriber's or the Publisher's end. Upon noticing the change, it moves incremental data to the rest of the participant servers. Merge Agent runs at the Distributor if configured for Push subscription, whereas it will run at the Subscriber if configured for Pull subscription. In Merge Replication, Merge Agent collects information about all of the undelivered row changes and assigns generation values that are higher than all previously generated values. These values are used to keep track of the highest generation values that need to be sent to various participant servers. The generation values are different for every server that is participant of the Merge Replication, and they are used to determine the order of changes.

- **Queue Reader Agent**: The Queue Reader Agent is used with the Transactional Replication, if configured with the Queued Updating. This agent's work is to move the updated or added data to the Publisher from the Subscriber. The Queue Reader Agent runs at the Distributor and there is only one Queue Reader Agent for all Publishers.

Prerequisites for Snapshot Replication

In the previous section, we saw that the Snapshot Replication is the basic and simplest replication topology. We should be very aware and familiar with the way Snapshot Replication can be implemented and the way it works. There is another reason for the need to be familiar with Snapshot Replication—even if we plan to implement Transactional or Merge Replication, the initial replication that gets applied is the Snapshot Replication. Therefore, we should be careful when we decide to design and implement replication solutions in our environment. There are a few prerequisites and considerations to be taken care of before implementing Snapshot Replication.

- **Primary Key**: Tables without a primary key cannot be considered for replication as per normalization rule. At the same time, the table without a primary key cannot be considered a candidate for being a part of replication by design.

- **Securing snapshot folder**: Snapshot folder is a folder that stores all the data that has been scheduled for replication. Replication agent will read and write data to this folder and so it is most important that we assign proper permission to the agent service account so that it can work error free. We should check the permission, by logging in and using the service account that has been configured to run the agent into the system, using and accessing the shared folder.

- **Schedule**: This point is very important as it talks about the schedule for executing the agent to read and write data to the snapshot folder and then applying it to one or more Subscriber server(s). If we have a large set of data, we should carefully configure the schedule so that it won't clash with the peak hours or does not hinder the performance during work hours.

- **Network bandwidth**: Network bandwidth is as equally an important point as securing and scheduling. We should have enough bandwidth allocated to the Subscriber and Publisher so that we do not have to worry about data when it is being transmitted over the network. If we have a slow or poorly performing network, we should work with a networking team to overcome an issue, as this may hinder not only the performance of the server but also of the whole network, especially when datasets are large.

Performance tuning tip:

We can split the snapshot into smaller chunks or a collection of objects so that we can improve the performance. It will be discussed in detail in *Appendix A, Troubleshooting*.

Installing

Let's get started with Snapshot Replication. In this section, we will learn how to install Snapshot Replication. We will later learn about various configuration options of Snapshot Replication.

The very first step is to create the Distributor server and distribution database so that we can set up the Publisher server and publication database on that.

Configuring Distributor and Publisher

Let's see how to configure the Distributor and Publisher step-by-step:

1. In the left pane of **SQL Server Management Studio** (SSMS), in the **Object Explorer** window, connect to the server we wish to set as Distributor. Once we are connected, right-click on **Replication Node**, select **Configure Distribution...**, and click **Next**.

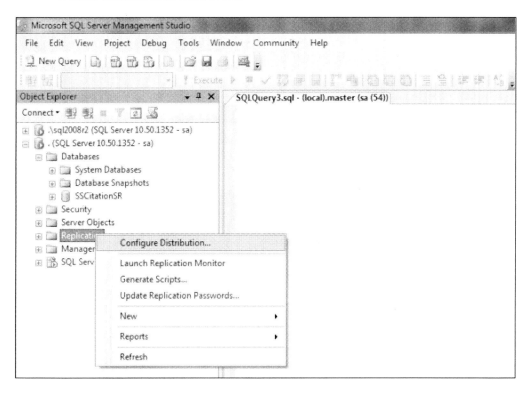

2. In the **Distributor** dialog box, we have two options:
   - Configure the current server as a Distributor.
   - We may add a server other than the current server by clicking on the **ADD** button.

After selecting the preferred option, click **Next**.

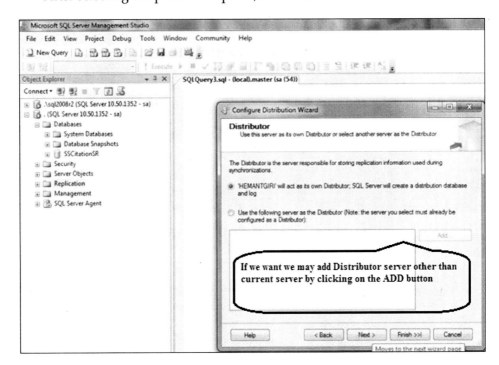

3. Here, the wizard will ask us whether it can configure the SQL Server Agent service to start automatically, if it is configured as disabled or manual. In case we have set the SQL Server Agent as manual, select **Yes, configure SQL Server Agent to start automatically**.

This step is encountered only if we have the SQL Server Agent service configured as **manual** or **disabled**.

4. In the Snapshot folder dialog box, provide the path of the network shared folder that we have procured to store the snapshot data — in our case, it is \\hemantgiri\share.

5. In the distribution database dialog box, we may change the name of distribution database; typically, we do keep the distribution database name intact. If required, we can change the name of Distributor database and we can also change the location for Distribution database files to a disk drive that has higher Disk I/O rate, which ultimately helps improve performance.

We can put the distribution database on a separate hardware RAID array, such as a separate RAID 10 array, to get a better performance.

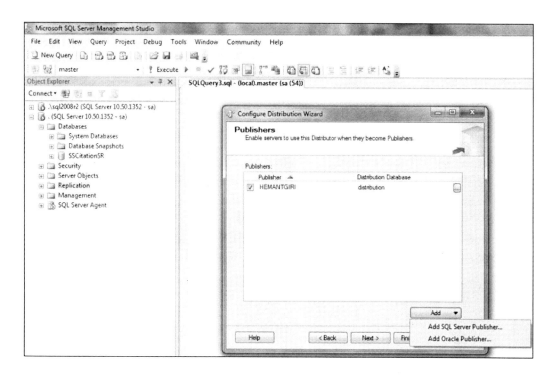

6. In the **Publishers** dialog box, we can see the server we selected to act as a Distributor earlier in step 3. If we wish, we can add the Publisher directly, by clicking on the **Add** button. When we click on the **Add** button, we have the option of having SQL Server or Oracle as a Publisher.

Having Oracle as a Publisher is a feature added since SQL Server 2005 was launched. We can add Oracle as a Publisher, provided it runs on Oracle 9i or onwards. This works in a similar way to how it works with SQL Server: Snapshot Agent connects to the Oracle server and creates schema script. The script is then stored in the snapshot share folder and, when the Snapshot Agent runs, it creates the set of data each time it is run.

This is generally useful when we migrate to SQL Server from Oracle database, when SQL Server has to act as a staging database, or while an application needs to access data from the non-SQL Server database.

7. In the wizard action dialog box, select **Configure distribution and Generate a script file** with steps to configure distribution and click **Next**.

8. In the script file properties, enter the location where we want to store the configure Distributor script and click **Next**.

9. In the **Complete the Wizard** dialog box, click **Finish**. This finishes the process of configuring Distributor.

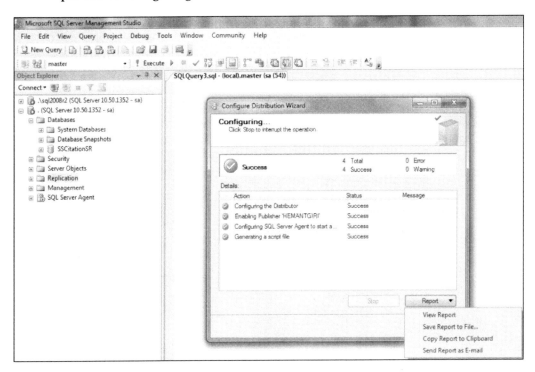

Let's take a look at the generated script.

```
/****** Scripting replication configuration. Script Date: 4/21/2010
3:18:15 PM ******/
Installing the server as a Distributor and Publisher
******/
use master
exec sp_adddistributor @distributor = N'HEMANTGIRI', @password = N''
GO
exec sp_adddistributiondb @database = N'distribution',
@data_folder = N'C:\Program Files\Microsoft SQL Server\MSSQL10_
50.MSSQLSERVER\MSSQL\Data',
@log_folder = N'C:\Program Files\Microsoft SQL Server\MSSQL10_
50.MSSQLSERVER\MSSQL\Data',
@log_file_size = 2,
-- Minimum days to retain distribution data
@min_distretention = 0,
-- Maximum days to retain distribution data
@max_distretention = 72,
-- History rentention days
@history_retention = 48,
@security_mode = 1
GO


use [distribution]
if (not exists (select * from sysobjects where name = 'UIProperties'
and type = 'U '))
    create table UIProperties(id int)
if (exists (select * from ::fn_listextendedproperty('SnapshotFolder',
'user', 'dbo', 'table', 'UIProperties', null, null)))
    EXEC sp_updateextendedproperty N'SnapshotFolder', N'\\hemantgiri\
share', 'user', dbo, 'table', 'UIProperties'
else
    EXEC sp_addextendedproperty N'SnapshotFolder', N'\\hemantgiri\
share', 'user', dbo, 'table', 'UIProperties'
GO


exec sp_adddistpublisher
-- Name of the publisher
@publisher = N'HEMANTGIRI',
-- Name of the Distribution database
@distribution_db = N'distribution',
-- Security mode, 0 = SQL Authentication and 1= Windows Authentication
@security_mode = 0,
-- Login name used
```

```
@login = N'sa',
-- Specify the password
@password = N'',
-- Shared folder
@working_directory = N'\\hemantgiri\share',
-- Trusted should be false always, this has been deprecated and used
only for backward compatibility
@trusted = N'false',
-- This value will be 1 when publisher is non-SQL Server
@thirdparty_flag = 0,
-- This can be either Oracle or Oracle Gateway if it is non-SQL Server
publisher
@publisher_type = N'MSSQLSERVER'
GO
```

This code will enable the Publisher and create a shared location for snapshot data with the SQL Server Authentication mode. Here, `@thirdparty_flag` defines if the publication is either Oracle or Oracle gateway.

Creating publication

Now that we have configured Distributor, it is time to create publication. Let's now create a publication.

1. Connect to the server on which we want to create publication. Right-click on the replication node and select **New Publication**.

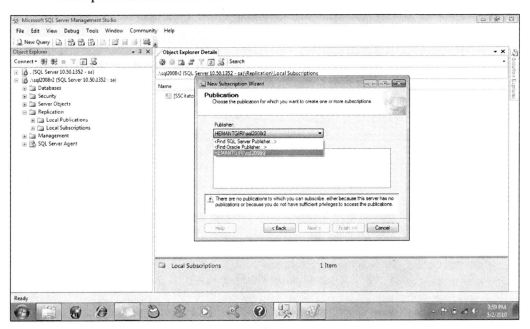

2. In the **New Publication Wizard** dialog box, click **Next**.

3. In the **Publication Database** dialog box, select the database that should act as a publication database and click **Next**.

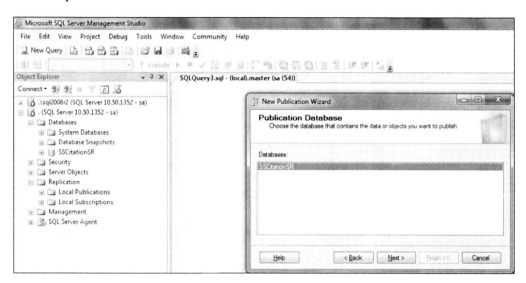

4. In the **Publication Type** database, select the type of publication and click **Next**.

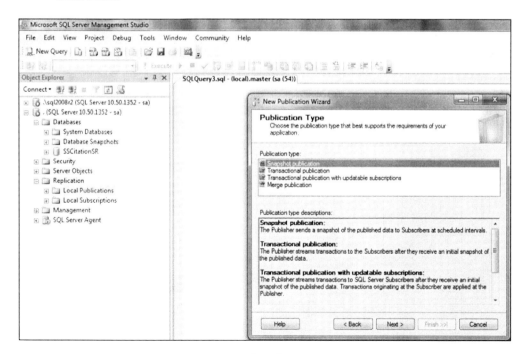

5. In the **Articles** dialog box, select the articles and/or stored procedure to replicate. Please note that only those tables that have a primary key will be listed here. Once we select article(s), click **Next**.

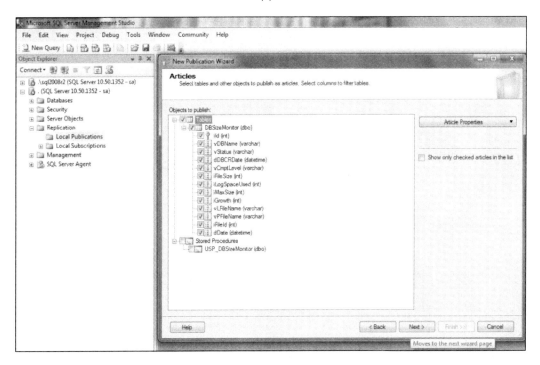

6. In the filter dialog box, we may add filter as per our business requirement. If we have any, click on the add button icon and we can filter records based on the WHERE condition.

7. In the **Filter statement** text area, look at the expression vDBName != [tempdb]. This expression means the record that has a database name other then tempdb will be replicated. Once we are done, click on the **OK** button to close the dialog box.

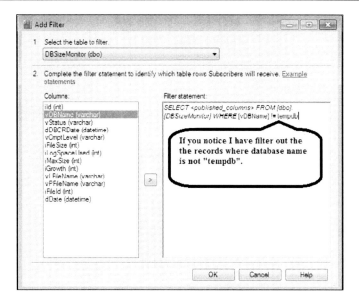

8. In the **Snapshot Agent** dialog box, select **Create snapshot immediately and keep the snapshot available to initialize subscription** and **Schedule the snapshot agent to run at the following times**. Click on the **Change...** button to change the schedule.

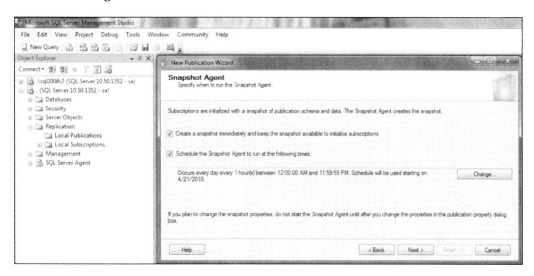

9. Upon clicking on the **Change...** button, we will see a screen like the one shown in the next screenshot, where we have to set the schedule according to our business environment and criticality. In this example, we have scheduled it to run at the interval of **20** minutes. Once we are done with scheduling, click **OK** and then **Next**.

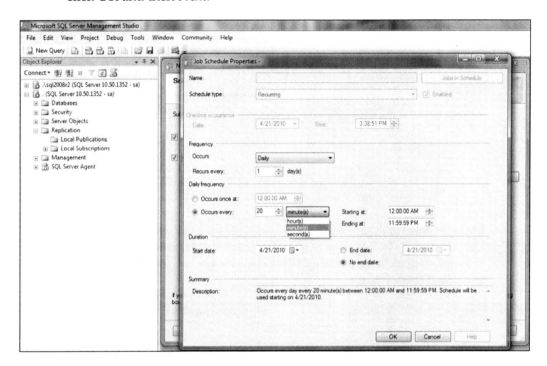

10. In the **Agent Security** dialog box, click **Settings**. This brings us to the following dialog box wherein we will have to specify the service account credential, although we can run it under SQL Server Agent service account. We should use a separate domain user (recommended) for the Snapshot Agent to run. While connecting to the Publisher, we can mention the SQL Server login or can impersonate the process account. Once we are done, click **OK** and then **Next**.

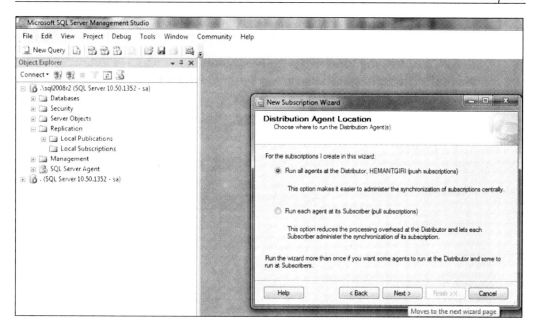

11. In the **Wizard Actions** dialog box, select **Create the publication** and
    Generate a script file with the steps to create the publication, and then
    click **Next**.

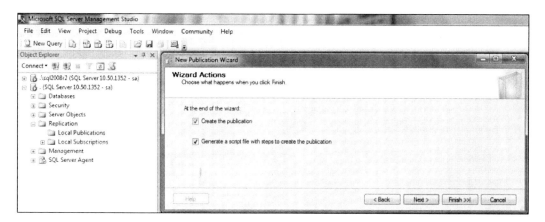

12. In the script file properties, mention the name and path where we want to keep the script and click **Next**.

13. In the **Complete the Wizard** dialog box, mention the name of the publication and verify that configurations are correct. Click **Finish**.

14. The next screen shows the result of every step we have been through the wizard while creating the publication. Please verify that the result displays success.

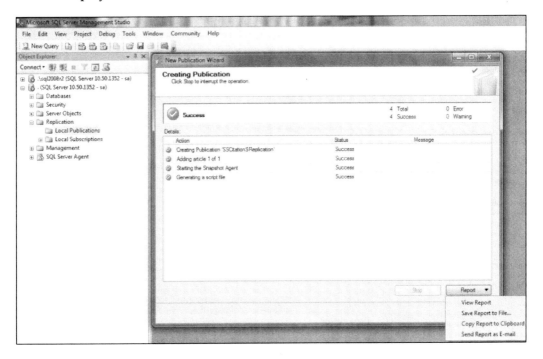

Let's have a look at what there is inside the script generated in step 21:

The following code will enable a database for the Publication:

```
use [SSCitationSR]
-- Enabling SSCitationSR database for publishing
exec sp_replicationdboption
@dbname = N'SSCitationSR',
@optname = N'publish',
@value = N'true'
GO
-- Adding the snapshot publication
use [SSCitationSR]
exec sp_addpublication
-- Name of the Publication
```

```
@publication = N'SSCitationSReplication',
@description = N'Snapshot publication of database ''SSCitationSR''
from Publisher ''HEMANTGIRI''.',
-- Publication Method
@sync_method = N'native',
-- Retention period for Subscription activity
@retention = 0,
-- Is Push subscription allowed, default is true
@allow_push = N'true',
-- Is Pull subscription allowed, default is false.
@allow_pull = N'false',
-- Anonymous subscription allowed? Default is false, if true
Immediate_subscription should be allowed to create anonymous
subscription
@allow_anonymous = N'true',
-- Is this publication enabled for internet
@enabled_for_internet = N'false',
-- Default value is true, it will store the replication files in
default folder if value is not set for an alternate folder
@snapshot_in_defaultfolder = N'true',
-- Should this snapshot be compressed, default false. If true it will
compress the files to reduce network overhead
@compress_snapshot = N'false',
-- Port number for FTP
@ftp_port = 21,
-- FTP Login ID, only useful when FTP is enable and used to send
snapshot file across
@ftp_login = N'anonymous',
-- Subscription copy is allowed or not, default is false.
@allow_subscription_copy = N'false',
-- Is added to active directory, default is false. Can integrate to
ADS to tighten the security.
@add_to_active_directory = N'false',
-- This option have to be Continuous if @Enabled_for_p2p, since we did
not enabled P2P it will have value Snapshot
@repl_freq = N'snapshot',
-- If status is active publication data is available for subscribers
immediately.
@status = N'active',
-- If true this will be the individual or stand-alone agent for this
particular publication. If false it will be shared agent with other
publication.
@independent_agent = N'true',
-- If immediate Synch is true it re-create snapshot each time agent
runs. If true, Indipendent_agent should be true.
-- Since we have single database and small publication, keep this both
value true is feasible
-- This is not recommended when articles in good numbers and snapshot
data is great in size
@immediate_sync = N'true',
```

```
-- Allows immediate updating subscriptions are allowed
@allow_sync_tran = N'false',
-- When @allow_sync_tran is true this option will be true, if false
this option will be false
@autogen_sync_procs = N'false',
-- Changes at the subscribers are not queued. True is not supported
for Oracle publishers.
@allow_queued_tran = N'false',
-- Publication allows DTS or not
@allow_dts = N'false',
-- Specifies if DDL are replicated, Default is 1 (true) means Schema
changes are allowed
@replicate_ddl = 1
GO
```

The following code will add Snapshot Publication:

```
exec sp_addpublication_snapshot
-- Name of publication
@publication = N'SSCitationSReplication',
-- By default the value is 4, this indicates that the frequency is
daily.
@frequency_type = 4,
-- Default is 4 (daily)
@frequency_interval = 4,
-- Is the date snapshot agent runs, default value is 1
@frequency_relative_interval = 1,
-- Specifies the recurrence value for frequency type, default value is
0
@frequency_recurrence_factor = 0,
-- Specify the unit of frequency, 4 indicates minutes
@frequency_subday = 4,
-- Interval for unit of frequency is 20, means every 20 minutes it
will be executed
@frequency_subday_interval = 20,
-- Indicates the start time, default is 0. Means starts at 00:00 hrs
@active_start_time_of_day = 0,
-- Indicates the end time, default is 0. Means starts at 23:59 hrs
@active_end_time_of_day = 235959,
-- Indicates the start date, default is 0. With 0 agent will start
when it is first configured.
@active_start_date = 0,
-- With the value 0, Agent will have no end date configured.
@active_end_date = 0,
-- Specifies the Agent job login, generally SQL Server Agent account
@job_login = null,
-- specifies the Agent job password
@job_password = null,
-- Specifies security mode used, default value is 1. 1 = Windows
authentication and 0=SQL authentication
@publisher_security_mode = 1
```

The following code will add articles to the Publication:

```
use [SSCitationSR]
exec sp_addarticle
-- Name of publication
@publication = N'SSCitationSReplication',
-- Name of article
@article = N'DBSizeMonitor',
-- Owner of source table
@source_owner = N'dbo',
-- Name of source object
@source_object = N'DBSizeMonitor',
-- Type logbased is default value
@type = N'logbased',
-- Description for an article
@description = null,
-- Should article schema be scripted, if not null should contain the
path for script
@creation_script = null,
-- Specifies that the article should be dropped if already exists,
drop is the default option.
@pre_creation_cmd = N'drop',
-- Generated based on the replication and article type
@schema_option = 0x000000000803509D,
-- Here we will mention the value for identity columns. If there is an
-- Identity value how should it be managed Manual or none or auto or
- null. If manual, it will set Not For Replication property on
@identityrangemanagementoption = N'manual',
-- Name of the destination table
@destination_table = N'DBSizeMonitor',
-- Owner of the destination table
@destination_owner = N'dbo',
-- Article is vertically partitioned or not
@vertical_partition = N'false'
GO
```

At this point, we have successfully configured distribution and publication; let's move ahead and create subscription.

Creating subscription

We have already created Distributor and Publisher, let's now create a subscription.

1. Connect to the server on which we want to create the subscription. Once we are connected, click on Replication node and select **Replication node | Local Subscription**. Then right-click and select **New Subscription**.

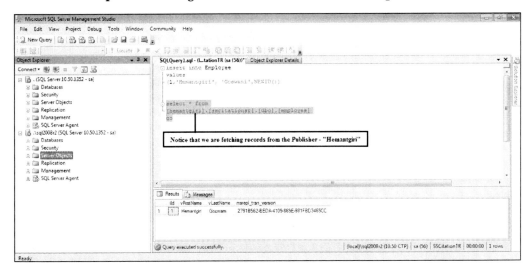

2. In the next screen, select the **New Subscription Wizard** and click **Next**.

3. In this step, we will have to connect to the Publisher server that we have just created.

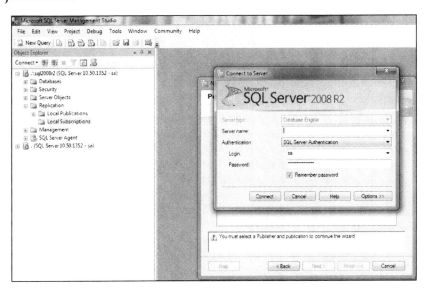

4. In the **Publication** dialog box, click on the database, select the publication, and click **Next**.

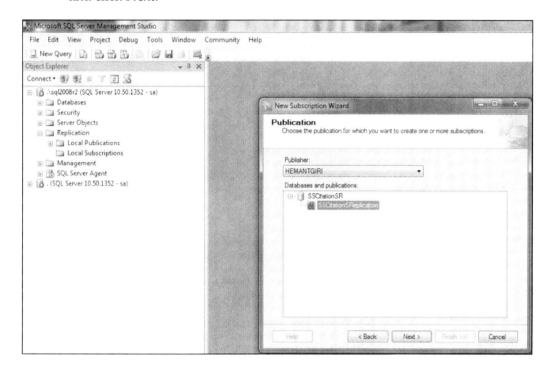

 We can have more than one publication on a single database.

5. In the **Distribution Agent Location**, select the appropriate option between: **Run all agents at the Distributor** (this will create push subscription) or **Run each agent at its Subscriber** (this will create pull subscription). In case we opt for push subscription, there will be a little overhead on the Distributor database, whereas in the case of pull subscription, overhead on the Distributor will be reduced.

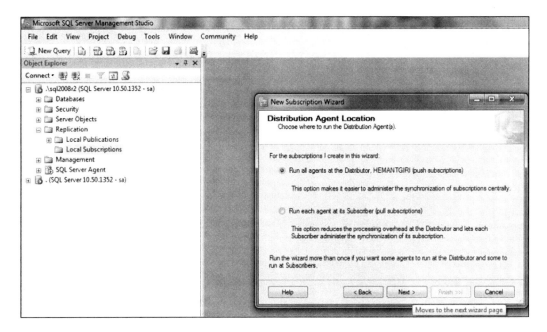

6. In the **Subscribers** dialog box, click on the drop-down and select the database we want to act as a Subscriber or we may create a new database. In our case, we will create a new database named SSCitationSR.

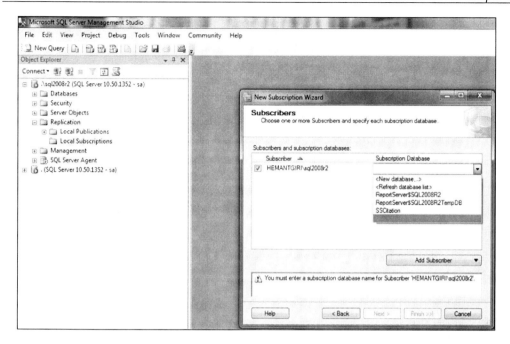

7. We may want to add another Subscriber if we wish by clicking on the **Add Subscriber** button at the bottom. This can be **SQL Server Subscriber** or a **Non-SQL Server Subscriber**.

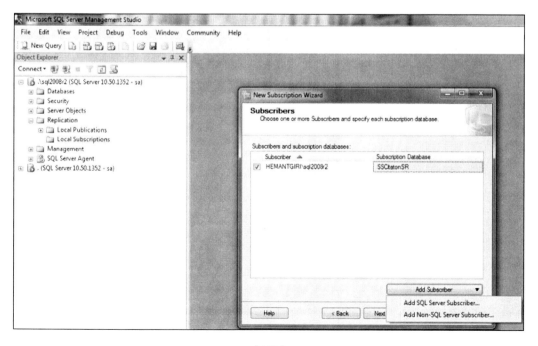

We can configure Oracle, IBM DB2 as a non-SQL server subscriber. Refer to the following link for more details: `http://technet.microsoft.com/en-us/library/ms151195.aspx`.

8. In the **Distribution Agent Security** dialog box, enter the credential we may want to use the agent to run on, which can be a domain user or a machine user. Although we can run the agent under the security context of the SQL Server Agent, it is not recommended. On the other hand, Distributor and Subscriber can be configured to run either under the SQL Server login or by impersonating the process account. Click **Next**.

 We should remember that the login we use to connect to Subscriber must be a database owner, and, on the Distributor, the process account must be a member of the publication access list.

9. In the **Synchronization Schedule** dialog box, specify the schedule for the agent to run. We can select either **Run continuously**, **Run on demand only**, or we can define it according to our requirement.

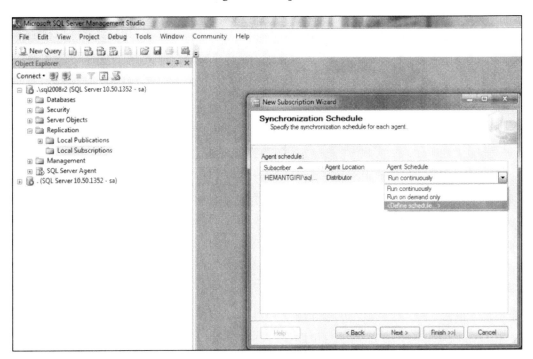

10. In the **Initialize Subscriptions** dialog box, we can select when to initialize subscription data using the **Initialize When** drop-down list. We can skip this if we already have the most recent backup copy restored at the Subscriber. We can notice a little checkbox; when checked, it will generate an initial dataset along with replication metadata and procedures, and when unchecked, it will generate only replication metadata and procedures. There are two options for the **Initialize When** option, they are:

   ○ **Immediately**: When this option is selected, subscription will get initialized immediately after the subscription wizard finishes.

   ○ **At First Synchronization**: If this option is selected, the initialization will occur the first time the agent runs.

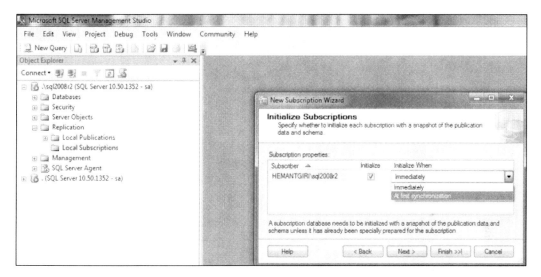

11. In the **Wizard Action** dialog box, select the options to create subscription(s) and generate a script file with the steps to create the subscription(s). Click **Next**.

12. In the **Script File Properties**, provide the name of the script file and a path to store the file. Click **Next**.

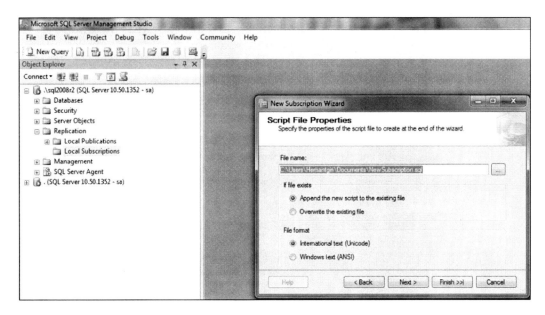

13. In the **Complete the wizard** dialog box, verify the correctness of the configuration we have provided so far. Click **Finish**.

The next code will add Subscription for the Snapshot Replication:

```
-----------------BEGIN: Script to be run at Publisher
'HEMANTGIRI'----------------
use [SSCitationSR]
-- This will add subscription
exec sp_addsubscription
-- Name of the publication
@publication = N'SSCitationSRReplication',
-- Name of the Subscriber
@subscriber = N'HEMANTGIRI\sql2008r2',
-- Destination DB Name
@destination_db = N'SSCitatonSR',
-- Subscription Type
@subscription_type = N'Push',
-- Specifies the synchronization type, default is Automatic. That
means schema and initial data are transferred to the subscriber
first
@sync_type = N'automatic',
-- Specifies that we have added all article for subscriber
@article = N'all',
```

```
-- Indicate the mode of update, if set to read only (default)
updates at subscriber are not sent to publisher
@update_mode = N'read only',
-- Type of subscriber, 0 is default value which means that
subscriber is SQL Server
@subscriber_type = 0
```

This code will create the Pull subscription agent for the Subscriber that we just have created with the help of the preceding code:

```
exec sp_addpullsubscription_agent
-- Name of the publication
@publication = N'SSCitationSReplication',
-- Subscriber name
@subscriber = N'HEMANTGIRI\sql2008r2',
-- Subscriber DB
@subscriber_db = N'SSCitatonSR',
@job_login = null,
@job_password = null,
-- Default is Null, if 1 is set the security mode is Windows
authentication and if set to 0 authentication mode is SQL
@subscriber_security_mode = 1,
-- Indicates the interval at agent should run, if set to 4 it runs
daily.
@frequency_type = 4,
-- Default value is 1, this value is set by the frequency type
@frequency_interval = 1,
-- Default value is 1
@frequency_relative_interval = 1,
@frequency_recurrence_factor = 1,
-- is a value of frequency, 4 means scheduled for daily
@frequency_subday = 4,
@frequency_subday_interval = 5,
@active_start_time_of_day = 0,
@active_end_time_of_day = 235959,
@active_start_date = 20100421,
@active_end_date = 99991231,
-- Subscription is not registered with Microsoft Synchronize
manager
@enabled_for_syncmgr = N'False',
@dts_package_location = N'Distributor'
GO
-----------------END: Script to be run at Publisher 'HEMANTGIRI'--
---------------
```

14. In the **Creating Subscription(s)...** dialog box, verify that every step returns a successful report; if not, please check the report, correct the error, and run the wizard again.

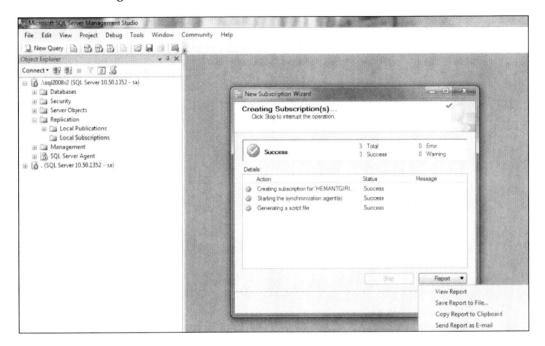

15. At this time, we have successfully configured Distributor, Publisher, and a Subscriber. Hovering the mouse over the **Local Subscription** node shows details of the Publisher, publication database, and publication name. It will also show the name of the Subscriber, subscription database, and the location of the Distribution Agent.

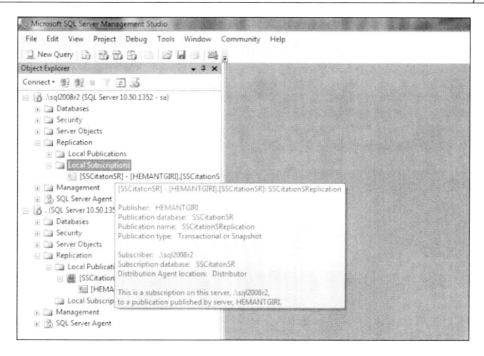

Configuring Snapshot Replication

While configuring, we have opted for the agent to run on the Distributor and hence it has created some agent jobs that keep replication working and alive. In the beginning of this chapter, we learned what the Snapshot Agent and the Distributor Agent are. Let's now have a look at what it takes to synchronize a database at the Subscriber end.

Snapshot Agent

The Snapshot Agent is an executable file—`snapshot.exe`. This file creates schema and data of published tables and data objects, and stores the files in the snapshot folder. It also has records of synchronization jobs in the distribution database.

Distribution Agent

It is an executable file—distrib.exe. Distribution agent is responsible for moving snapshot and transactions (for Transactional Replication) to the Subscribers.

When we configured replication, it creates an agent and its profiles get created. Generally, an agent profile has a set of parameters, that are queried each time an agent runs and logs into the Distributor. Apart from agents, it creates some maintenance jobs to keep the database synchronized and in shape. Refer to the following screenshot:

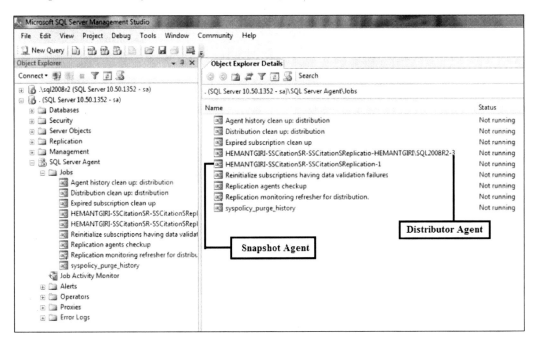

Maintenance jobs

When we configure replication, it creates some jobs that ensure the smooth functioning of replication. Here is a brief introduction to these jobs.

Agent history clean up: distribution

This job will remove replication agent history from the distribution database. By default, this job runs every ten minutes.

Distribution clean up: distribution

This job will remove replicated transactions from the distribution database. It also verifies whether subscription is synchronized with the maximum retention period. If maximum retention period exceeds, it will deactivate the subscription. By default, this job runs every ten minutes.

Expired subscription clean up

This job will verify if the subscription is expired. If it is, it will remove it from the publication database.

Reinitialize subscriptions having data validation failures

This job will mark subscription to be reinitialized and applies the new snapshot if it is found that the subscription has failed during data validation.

Replication agents check-up

This job will monitor replication agents; if agents are not logging history, it will make an entry in to a Windows event log if a job fails.

Replication monitoring refresher for distribution

This job will refresh cached queries that are used by Replication Monitor.

Let's have a look at some properties of publication. As a constraint, we cannot cover each and every property, but I would certainly cover those that need attention.

Expand the replication node, expand the Local Publications, right-click on **Publication Name**, and select **Properties**. This will bring the following screen. We can see lots of options on the left-hand side of the dialog box. Click on **General** and it will populate general information on the right-hand side pane.

Configuring publication properties

On the **Publication Properties** screen, we can see the publication **Name, Database, Description, Type** (of replication), and **Subscription expiration**. Based on the business demand, we should decide the retention period for subscription. If we select the **Subscriptions expire and may be dropped if not synchronized in the following number of hours** option, this will drop the subscription if it exceeds the interval, which is really dangerous. Instead, choose the **Subscription never expires but they can be deactivated until they are reinitialized** option.

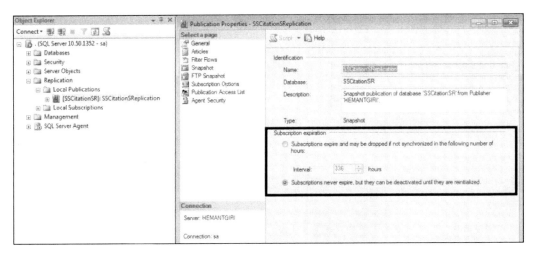

Click **Articles** on the left-hand side of the dialog box and click on the **Article Properties** button, which populates the screen as shown in the next screenshot. If we look carefully, we will notice that it contains detailed information on what should be copied along with data, namely extended properties, constraints, and so on while replicating an article. We should wisely modify this property, if required.

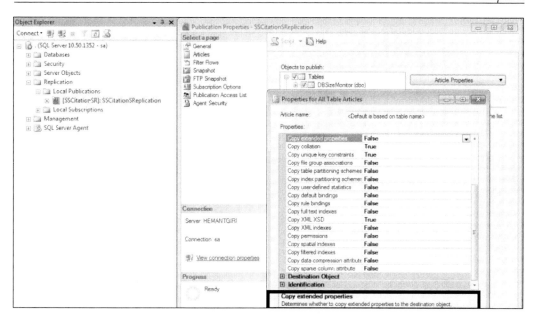

When we click on the snapshot folder, we will see the following screen that shows the options such as **Snapshot format**, **Location of snapshot files**, and **Run additional scripts**. The most noticeable thing is the **Compress snapshot files in this folder** option. If this option is selected, it will store snapshot files in the compressed mode. This will make the process faster, as it will reduce the time it takes to traverse through a network.

Although this helps improve performance, we should be cautious while using this option. This is because all the files are first compressed, they will then traverse to the shared location on the network, and will get decompressed again to get restored to the Subscriber. So, we should test this option thoroughly before implementing it into the production.

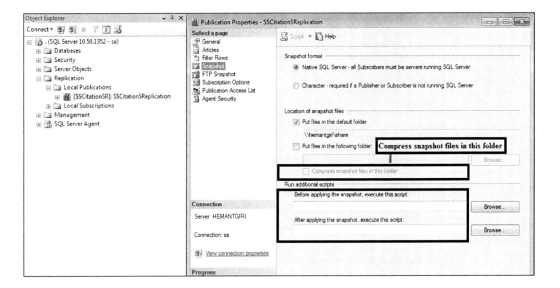

When we click on the Subscription options, it will show the following screen. The most important thing to consider is **Schema Replication**. We should be cautious because when set the **Replicate Schema changes** option to **True**, it will replicate *Alter Table*, *Alter View*, *Alter Procedure*, *Alter Function*, and *Alter Trigger* commands.

If we drop a column from a published article, it will drop the column from the Subscribers, even if we have set the **Replication Schema Changes** option to **False**.

It is not recommended to use **SQL Server Management Studio (SSMS)** to make changes. This is because in the previous code, SSMS drops and recreates the object, and as we cannot drop the published article without removing it from publication, schema changes will fail. This is why it is recommended to use the command-line mode to make changes to the existing publication or Subscriber.

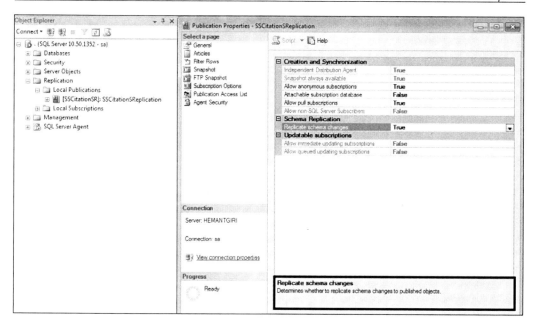

Configuring alerts

Right-click on the publication node of the Publisher server and select **Replication Monitor**. This will launch Replication Monitor. Replication Monitor is a very handy tool to configure various options for replication and troubleshooting. Using replication monitor, we can also configure alerts. The following are the steps to create alerts:

1. To launch the RM, right-click on the publication node and select RM. Alternatively, we can call `sqlmonitor.exe` directly to launch RM.

2. Expand **My Publisher | Publisher Name | Publication Name**. Select the **Warning** tab in the right-hand pane.

3. Click on the **Configure alerts** to bring up the following screen, as shown in the next screenshot.

4. Pick one of the alert types that we want to configure, for example, we have selected **Replication Agent Failure**.

5. Select the appropriate values in the **Replication agent failure** alert properties dialog box.

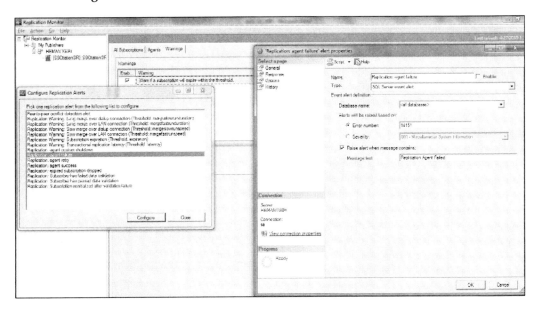

6. Select **Options**. Here, we may select a job to be executed for the next course of action and/or we can select **send Email or Pager** or **Net Send under Notify Operator**.

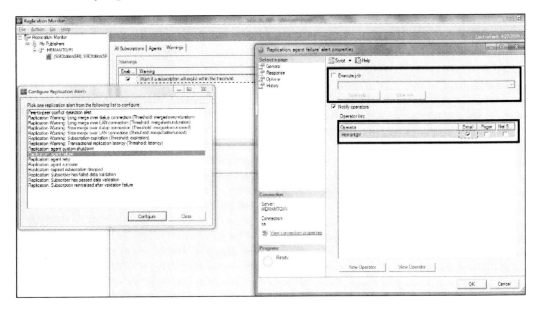

Snapshot Agent parameters

The following screenshot shows the Snapshot Agent parameters:

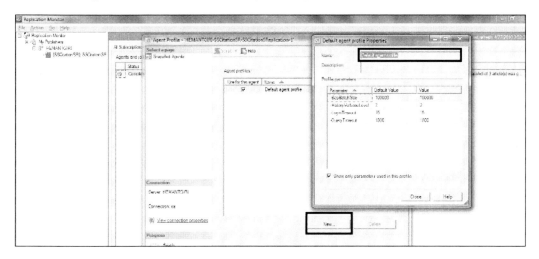

There are mainly four parameters that we will be focusing on.

- **-BcpBatchSize**: The value for this parameter defines the number of rows that can be sent in a bulk copy operation. While performing bcp, the batch size is the number of rows to send in a single transaction and the number of rows must be sent before the distribution agent logs a bcp message, whereas the fixed size of 1000 rows are used with bcp out.

- **-HistoryVerboseLevel**: This simply indicates the kind of logging that has happened with each value.

  - 0: This value means progress messages are written either to console or to an output file and are not recorded in the distribution database.

  - 1: This value means it will always update a previous history message of the same status. If no previous record exists, it will insert a new record.

  - 2: This is the default value. This will insert the new history records, unless the record is for things such as idle or long-running job.

  - 3: This value always inserts new records, unless it is for an idle message.

- **-LoginTimeout**: This value indicates the seconds before the login timeout occurs.

- **-QueryTimeout**: Indicates the number of seconds before the query times out.

Adding and dropping an article and a column to the existing publication using T-SQL

It is recommended to use T-SQL statements while we make any changes to the existing publication or while adding and dropping an article. Here is the sample code for adding and dropping an article and column to an existing publication:

```
use SSCitationSR
go
create table tbl_Employee
(
iId                      int primary key,
vFirstName               varchar(15),
vLastName        varchar(15),
vAddress         varchar(35),
vCity                    varchar(15),
vZip                     varchar(9)
)
go
```

Let's declare the system variable to store values for the replication:

```
DECLARE @publication AS sysname;
DECLARE @table AS sysname;
DECLARE @filterclause AS nvarchar(500);
DECLARE @filtername AS nvarchar(386);
DECLARE @schemaowner AS sysname;
DECLARE @forceinvalidatesnapshot as int;
-- This will set the value for Publication
SET @publication = N'SSCitationSReplication';
-- This will set the value for an article to be added
SET @table = N'tbl_Employee';

-- This will set the value for the filter
SET @filterclause = N'[iId] IS NULL';
-- This will be the name of the filter
SET @filtername = N'woiId';
-- This will set the name for the schema owner
SET @schemaowner = N'DBO';
-- If we set the value as 1 this will force snapshot to be invalidate
SET @forceinvalidatesnapshot = 1;
```

The following code will add an article to an existing publication with the filter clause:

```
EXEC sp_addarticle
    @publication = @publication,
    @article = @table,
    @source_object = @table,
    @source_owner = @schemaowner,
    @vertical_partition = N'true',
    @type = N'logbased',
    @filter_clause = @filterclause;
-- Add all columns to the article.
EXEC sp_articlecolumn
    @publication = @publication,
    @article = @table;
-- Removes the column vLastName from the article, change the @
operation = N'Add' will add a column
EXEC sp_articlecolumn
    @publication = @publication,
    @article = @table,
    @column = N'vLastName',
    @operation = N'drop';
-- As the article has filter clause call sp_articleview stored
procedure
-- vertical filtering view. Since the type is 'log based',
EXEC sp_articleview
    @publication = @publication,
    @article = @table,
    @filter_clause = @filterclause;
GO
--Add a pull subscription to a snapshot publication.
USE [SSCitationSR]
EXEC sp_addsubscription
  @publication = 'SSCitationSReplication',
  @subscriber = [hemantgiri\sql2008r2],
  @destination_db = 'SSCitationSR',
  @subscription_type = N'pull';
Go
```

As we have existing pull subscription, we have to execute `sp_refreshsubscription`, so that it will create a new snapshot for the existing pull subscription for the newly added article and not for every article. We should also remember that this stored procedure needs to be run at the Publisher end.

```
sp_refreshsubscriptions @publication ='SSCitationSReplication'
go
```

 All this code needs to be executed at the Publisher's end.

Summary

In this chapter, we learned about the replication in general and replication components. We have had a brief introduction to the different types of replication and jobs that each of them creates in order for replication to run smoothly. We discussed, step-by-step, how to configure Distributor, Publisher, and Subscriber for Snapshot Replication. In the next chapter, we will learn about Transactional Replication.

4
Transactional Replication

XY Incorporation is a mid-size manufacturing company, having its manufacturing unit in city A, while the management staff occupies their headquarters in city B. Both the offices are connected with the secured VPN tunnel of 2 MBPS. Management often complains of having a problem with the report module of the ERP application—the reports aren't created as quickly in city B as they are in the manufacturing plant.

XY Incorporation has its data centre located in city A, where it has two production database servers and uses database backups as a source of any emergency situation. The server being talked about here is maintained by the system administrator. Mr. Young had recently joined this company as a DBA, and management asked him to fine tune the reports so that they appear fast. While studying a system diagram, Mr. Young noticed that there is no HA configured here. He then approached the management saying that if the management has no problem with some latency, say 15 minutes (means near real time data for the reports), then he has a solution that serves their needs. He suggested to them that they implement Transactional Replication so that the report module connects to the separate server and thus load is shared. Also, because of the sharing of data, the data is available on another server and thus the management has another server ready to maintain High Availability. Let's now turn our attention to the Transactional Replication.

In the previous chapter, we learned about the Snapshot Replication. This chapter will focus on Transactional Replication, including:

- Prerequisites for implementing Transactional Replication
- A step-by-step installation of Transactional Replication
- Configuring Transactional Replication using T-SQL

There are some points that will need to be repeated. So, instead of repeating the content again, we will just have a reference to it.

Prerequisites for Transactional Replication

Just like Snapshot Replication, Transactional Replication too has some prerequisites to follow before we install and configure it. Let's have a look at the prerequisites for Transactional Replication.

- **Primary Key:** This is a basic rule that every article should have a Primary Key to be a candidate table for Transactional Replication.

  Primary keys are used to maintain uniqueness of records and to maintain referential integrity between tables, and that is why it is recommended for every article to have a primary key.

- **Securing snapshot folder:** This is about securing and accessing snapshot folder (please refer to the prerequisite section of *Chapter 3, Snapshot Replication*, for more details).

- **Schedule**: This is about scheduling the agent and jobs (please refer to the prerequisite section of Chapter 3 for more details).

- **Network bandwidth**: This talks about network bandwidth, which again has been discussed in the prerequisites section of Chapter 3.

- **Enough disk space for database being published**: We need to make sure that we have ample space available for the transaction log for the published database, as it will continue to grow and won't truncate the log records until they are moved to the distribution database. Please note that even in simple recovery model, the log file can grow large if replication breaks. That is the reason it is recommended to set T-log's auto grow option to value "true". We should also make sure that the distribution database is available and log reader agent is running.

- **Enough disk space for distribution database**: It is necessary to have enough disk space allocated to the distribution database. This is because the distribution database will store the transactions marked for replication until it is applied to the subscriber database within the limit of retention period of distribution (which is 72 hours by default), or it will retain the transactions until the snapshot agent re-runs and creates a new snapshot.

- **Use domain account as service account**: We should always use the domain account as a service account, so that when agents access the shared folder of snapshot files, it won't have any problem just because they are local to the system and do not have permission to access network share. While mentioning service account, we are asked to choose from two built-in accounts including **Local System account**, **Network Services**, and this account, wherein we have to specify the domain account on which the service account will run.

 For more information on service account types and selecting account, refer to the *External resources* section of this chapter.

Working with Transactional Replication

In the previous chapter, we learned how replication works, in general and in brief. Let's have a look at how the Transactional Replication works in detail. Consider a case wherein we need to have an exact replica of the database for reporting purposes at some remote location, and a latency of an hour is acceptable. Hence, we go for Transactional Replication.

1. Application/end user writes data to the database.
2. Snapshot agent prepares the schema and data of the published objects, and stores them in file format into the snapshot folder — this is called initial snapshot.
3. Log Reader agent keeps monitoring transaction logs, and copies the transactions (these are incremental changes) that are marked for replication into the distribution database.
4. At this time, distribution agent applies initial snapshot to the Subscriber.
5. Transactions that are marked for replication are applied to the Subscriber.

Installing Transactional Replication

In this section we will learn how to install Transactional Replication using wizard and using T-SQL. We will also learn about which account should be used to run SQL Server Agent.

Creating new publication for Transactional Replication

Let's start installing transactional replication by creating a new publication.

1. We need to connect to the server on which we want to create publication. Expand the replication node, right-click on **Local Publication**, and select **New Publication**.

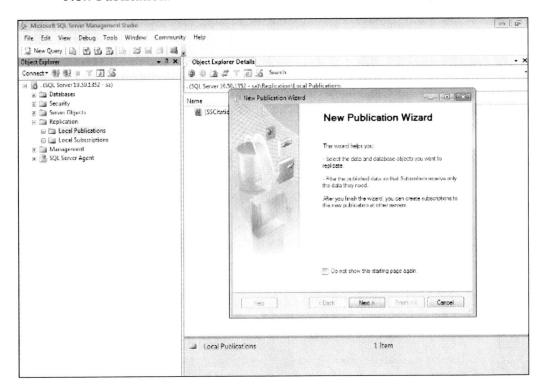

2. In the **Publication Database** dialog box, select the database to be published.

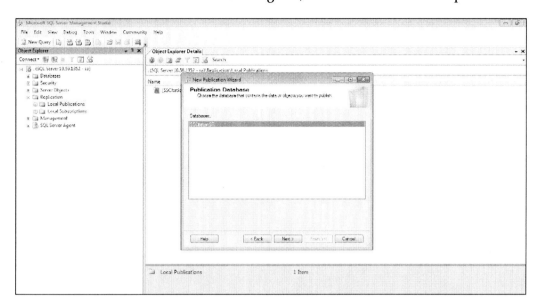

3. In the **Publication Type** dialog box, select the **Transactional replication**.

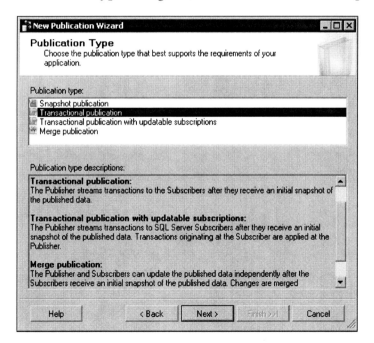

As seen in the screenshot, there two subtypes of Transactional Replication: **Transactional publication** and **Transactional publication with updatable subscriptions**.

The Transactional publication with updatable subscriptions subtype allows changes to be applied at the publisher's end based on the type of subscriptions—immediate updating or queued updating. We may switch between update types easily (we will cover this in the *Configuring Transactional Replication* section of this chapter).

> Updatable subscriptions that are featured will be removed in the next version of SQL Server; hence we should avoid using this feature in the production environment.

4. In the **Article Issues** dialog box, select the tables and stored procedures we may want to publish and then click **Next**.

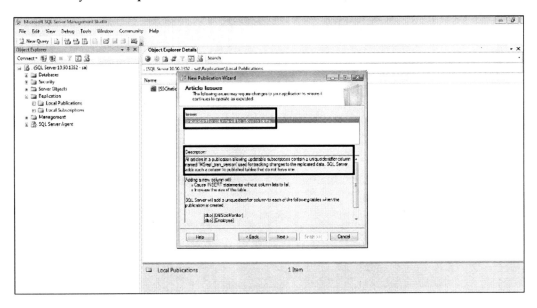

5. In the filter table rows, add the filter (if any) and click **Next**.

6. In the **Snapshot Agent** dialog box, specify the schedule for snapshot agent to run and click **Next**.

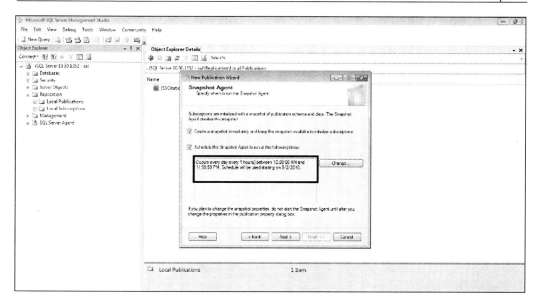

7. In the **Agent Security** dialog box, assign the snapshot agent account credential, we have opted to run it under **SQL Server Agent account**.

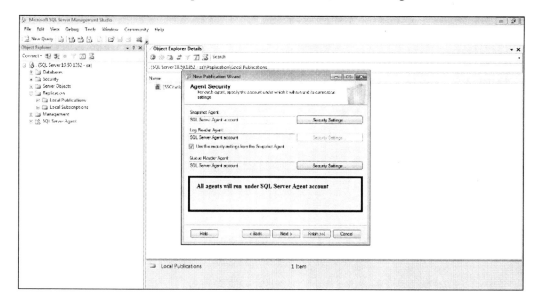

8. In the wizard actions, select **Create the publications and Generate a script file with code** to create the publication and click **Next**.

9. In the **Complete the Wizard** dialog box, give an appropriate name to the publication and click **Next**.

10. In the **Creating Publication** dialog box, verify that there is no error reported.

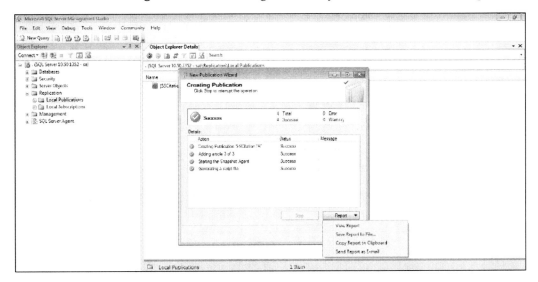

Creating subscription for Transactional Replication

As we have created the publication, let's move ahead and create the subscription.

1. Connect to the server we wish to create subscription on, expand the replication node, right-click on the **Local Subscriptions** option, and select **New Subscription**.

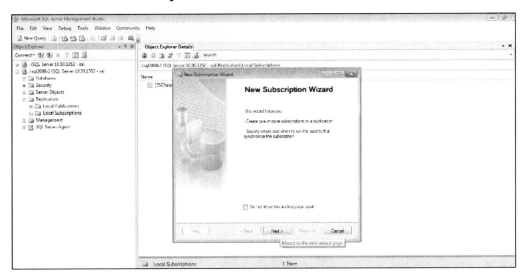

2. In the **Publication** dialog box, select the Publisher we have created previously and click **Next**.

3. Upon selecting the Publisher, we will be asked to choose the publication. Here, both the publications are available—snapshot and transactional. We will select the transactional publication we have just created and click **Next**.

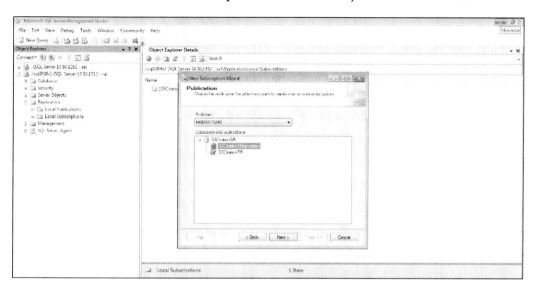

4. In the **Distribution Agent Location** dialog box, select the location where we want to run the distribution agent. We will select the **Run each agent as its Subscriber** option, which will create the pull subscription.

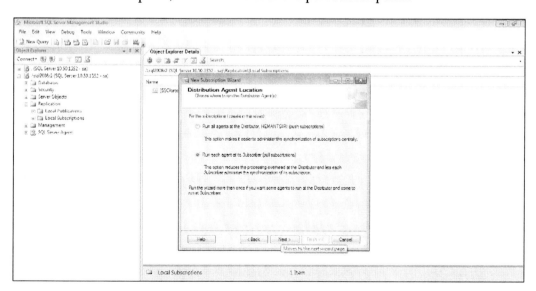

5. In the **Subscribers** dialog box, select the subscription database from the existing one; we may create a new database if we wish.

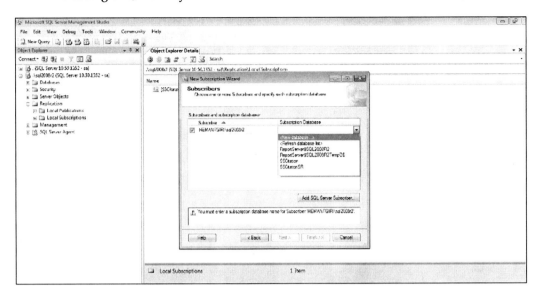

6. In the **Subscribers** dialog box, notice that we have created a new database. Also, note that we can add a new Subscriber if we wish to by clicking on the **Add SQL Server Subscriber** button at the bottom. Click **Next** once we are done.

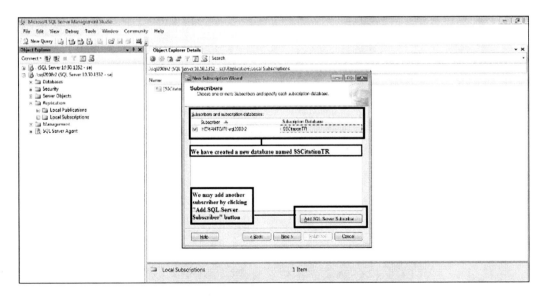

7. In the **Distribution Agent Security** dialog box, we have to specify the connection options to connect to the Distributor and to the Subscriber. In this case, we have selected the **Impersonate process account** option.

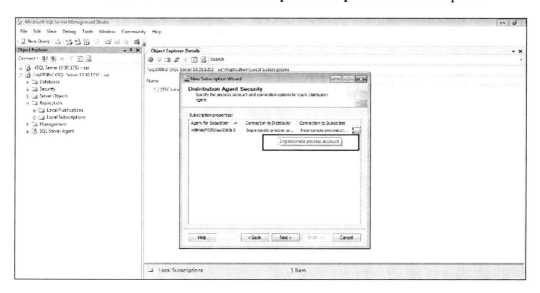

8. In the **Synchronization Schedule** dialog box, specify the schedule to run agent. We have configured it to run daily, on an hourly basis. Click **Next**.

9. In the **Updatable Subscriptions** dialog, choose when to commit the data changes to the Publisher and other Subscriber; we have selected the **Queue changes and commit when possible** option.

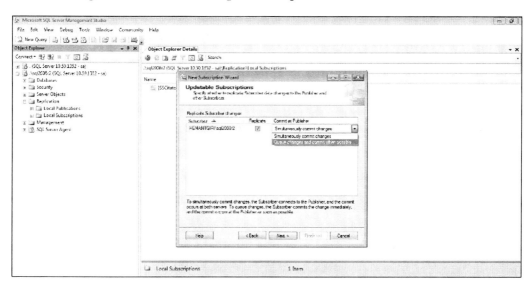

10. In the **Login for Updatable Subscriptions** dialog box, specify the login used to connect to the publisher; we may choose linked server or remote server if we have already created.

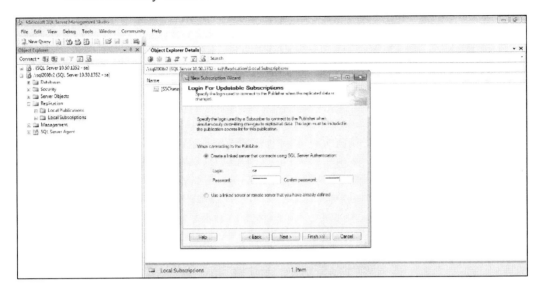

11. In the **Initialize Subscriptions** section, specify when to initialize the subscriptions—**immediately** or **At first synchronization**.

We need to be careful while selecting the initialization option. If we have recent backup of the database for which we are going to set up the replication, then we don't need to check the **Initialize** option and this will save a lot of time and resources that would have been occupied. But in case we do not have backup restored over the subscriber, we will need to check the **Initialize** option. There are two options available:

- ○ **Immediately:** This will initialize the synchronization as soon as the subscription wizard finishes

- ○ **At first synchronization:** This option will initialize synchronization the first time the agent runs

12. In the next dialog box, we will be asked to choose what to do when we click on **Finish**. Choose **Create the subscription** and **generate a script file with the steps to create the subscription** and click **Next**.

13. In the **Complete the wizard** dialog box, verify that the options we have selected are correct and click **Next**.

14. In the **Creating Subscription(s)...** dialog box, verify that it returns the success report.

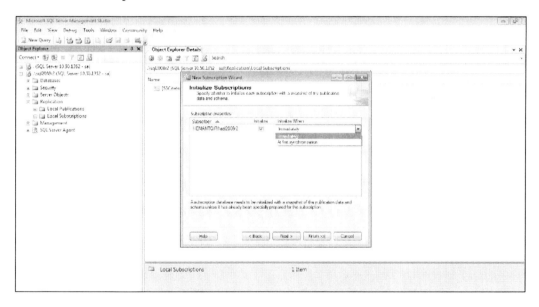

As we have updatable subscription, we need to make sure that the MS DTC service is running on the subscriber. This service is responsible to write data changes into the queue. This queue will then be read and delivered to the Publisher by Queue Reader Agent.

At this point, we have successfully created the Transaction Replicational with the updatable subscription using GUI. Now let's understand what if we have to create publication and subscription using T-SQL! We will make use of the scripts that are generated by the wizard, for us to be able to easily understand how it is configured.

Installing publication and subscription using T-SQL

We have learned how to install publication using SQL Server Management Studio. Let's now see how to install Transactional Replication using T-SQL. The following code will enable the database for the publication. We have to specify the name of the database and a value as `true`.

```
use [SSCitationSR]

exec sp_replicationdboption
@dbname = N'SSCitationSR',
@optname = N'publish',
@value = N'true'
GO
```

The following code will create the reader agent that will read the transactions to be published:

```
use [SSCitationSR]
exec [SSCitationSR].sys.sp_addqreader_agent
@job_login = null,
@job_password = null,
@job_name = null, @frompublisher = 1
GO
```

The following code will create publication for the given database:

```
use [SSCitationSR]
exec sp_addpublication
-- the name of the publication
@publication = N'SSCitationTR',
@description = N'Transactional publication with updatable
subscriptions of database ''SSCitationSR'' from Publisher
''HEMANTGIRI''.',
@sync_method = N'concurrent',
@retention = 0,
@allow_push = N'true',
@allow_pull = N'true',
@allow_anonymous = N'true',
```

```
@enabled_for_internet = N'false',
@snapshot_in_defaultfolder = N'true',
@compress_snapshot = N'false',
@ftp_port = 21,
@ftp_login = N'anonymous',
@allow_subscription_copy = N'false',
@add_to_active_directory = N'false',
@repl_freq = N'continuous',
@status = N'active',
@independent_agent = N'true',
@immediate_sync = N'true',
@allow_sync_tran = N'true',
@autogen_sync_procs = N'true',
@allow_queued_tran = N'true',
@allow_dts = N'false',
@conflict_policy = N'pub wins',
@centralized_conflicts = N'true',
@conflict_retention = 14,
@queue_type = N'sql',
@replicate_ddl = 1,
@allow_initialize_from_backup = N'false',
@enabled_for_p2p = N'false',
@enabled_for_het_sub = N'false'
GO
```

While writing the previous code, there are some options we should be careful with while configuring. They are:

- `@sync_method`: Choose **Concurrent** here. This means it will create a native-mode bulk copy output of all tables without locking them.

- `@retention`: This value defines the retention period of the subscription activity. The value of `0` indicates that the subscription never expires. It is recommended to define a retention period based on our environment.

- `@conflict_policy`: The value that we have defined here will denote who should win in case of a conflict. We need to choose this option wisely. This following code will create a snapshot agent for the publication we have just created. Here, we will specify the frequency type (daily or weekly), interval, start and end date, and time for the snapshot agent.

```
exec sp_addpublication_snapshot
@publication = N'SSCitationTR',
@frequency_type = 4,
@frequency_interval = 1,
@frequency_relative_interval = 1,
```

```
    @frequency_recurrence_factor = 0,
    @frequency_subday = 8,
    @frequency_subday_interval = 1,
    @active_start_time_of_day = 0,
    @active_end_time_of_day = 235959,
    @active_start_date = 0,
    @active_end_date = 0,
    @job_login = null,
    @job_password = null,
    @publisher_security_mode = 1
```

In the following code, we will be adding an article to the existing publication using the sp_addarticle system stored procedure. Using the same code, we can add more tables; the things we need to change are the article name and destination table name.

```
use [SSCitationSR]
exec sp_addarticle
@publication = N'SSCitationTR',
@article = N'DBSizeMonitor',
@source_owner = N'dbo',
@source_object = N'DBSizeMonitor',
@type = N'logbased',
@description = null,
@creation_script = null,
@pre_creation_cmd = N'drop',
@schema_option = 0x0000000008035CDF,
@identityrangemanagementoption = N'manual',
@destination_table = N'DBSizeMonitor',
@destination_owner = N'dbo',
@status = 16,
@vertical_partition = N'false'
GO
```

Configuring Transactional Replication

In the previous section of the chapter, we learned how to install Transactional Replication using wizard and using T-SQL. In this section, we will learn how to configure Transactional Replication using T-SQL and/or wizard so that we can have performance benefit.

Parameters to be configured with Distribution Agent profile

There are some parameters that can be customized according to the requirement and can help increase the performance of the replication. These parameters include:

- **Large Object (LOB) data types**: Transactional Replication supports LOB to get published. Whenever there is a change recorded in the LOB, it actually updates only fragments of the changed data and not the whole data. We should set the parameter value for `UseOledbStreaming`, `-OledbStreamThreshold`, and `-PacketSize` in the Distribution Profile for OLEDB streaming.

  All the options that we have referred to previously can be configured in the Distribution Agent profile. There is a pre-defined profile that we can use while dealing with the LOB data types — **Distribution Profile for OLEDB Streaming**.

    - `-UseOledbStreaming`: This option allows binding of binary large object as a stream.

    - `-OledbStreamThreshold`: Here we have to specify the threshold value. The objects that touch the threshold values are considered as a stream. This value varies from 400 to 1048576.

    - `-PacketSize`: The default value of packet size is 4096 bytes. We may increase or decrease based on our requirement.

    - `-QueryTimeout`: We may change the value of this parameter in case the transaction size is large and there is a chance that the timeout may occur before it gets applied over Subscriber. However, we need to be cautious with the value we specify.

 Be cautious when changing a packet size; it is better to work with our network team before we change the value here.

- SkipErrors: Whenever distribution agent encounters an error, it stops working. If we use the -SkipErrors parameter, the distribution agent will continue working after logging error. There is a pre-defined Distribution Agent profile titled *Continue on Data Consistency Errors*. It has three values, 2601, 2627, and 20598, and has been preconfigured for the -SkipErrors parameter. These three error codes have the following meaning:

  ○ 2601: Ignore the error **cannot insert duplicate key row in object**.

  ○ 2627: Violation of constraint, cannot insert duplicate key in object.

  ○ 20598: The row was not found at the subscriber when applying the replicated command.

- **Switching between update types:** Transactional Replication gives us flexibility of switching between update modes—immediate or queued update. This is extremely helpful in case network connectivity suffers. If we switch from immediate updating to queue updating, we cannot switch back to immediate updating until Queue Reader Agent has applied all of the pending messages in the queue. The following are the steps we have to follow, in order to change update type:

  i. Execute sp_helppullsubscription in case of pull subscription and sp_helpsubscription for push subscription—if the value of update mode in the result set is 3 or 4, failover is supported. Looking at the following result pane, we notice that the value of update_mode is **3**, indicating that failover is supported. This further means we don't need to execute the code mentioned next. In case it is other than 3 or 4, execute the code mentioned in the step ii.

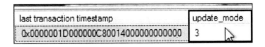

  ii. At the subscription database, execute sp_setreplfailovermode.

```
Sp_setreplfailovermode
@publisher = 'Hemantgiri',
@publisher_db='SSCitationSR',
@Publication='SSCitationTR',
@failover_mode='Queued'
```

  OR

```
Sp_setreplfailovermode
@publisher = 'Hemantgiri',
@publisher_db='SSCitationSR',
@Publication='SSCitationTR',
@failover_mode='Immediate'
```

There are some points that we should take into consideration when we configure Transactional Replication, so that we can reduce some overhead and gain the performance benefit:

- In case we need to have triggers in our database based on business requirements, we should set its property to **Not for Replication**. The same is true with the constraints such as Foreign key, Check constraints, and Identity columns.

- There are two ways to configure these options:
    - ° We can modify the existing object in the publication and/or subscription.
    - ° While adding an article using `sp_addarticle`, we can specify value for `@schema_option`.

- Schedule agents to run continuously.

- Configure distribution database on separate server.

- Minimize the retention period.

- In the agent profile, configure `-MaxBCPThreads` # equal to the number of articles.

- If the number of articles are large in number, we can always split them in two or more publications to reduce the overhead.

- Avoid horizontal partitioning, if feasible.

Summary

In this chapter we learned what Transactional Replication is, how it works, and the different prerequisites that we need to be careful of before we actually start installing Transactional Replication. We also learned how to configure Transactional Replication using T-SQL commands.

5
Merge Replication

Mr. Young is working as a Principal DBA with XY Incorporation, which is a large manufacturing company. XY Incorporation has their sales offices and manufacturing units spread across various countries, and they have their central database server located at their data center in Portland, Oregon. Sometimes they feel that the server is not producing reports in time, and sometimes they have problems accessing data when many people are accessing data from more than one location. So, when management asked Mr. Young to overcome this issue, he came up with an idea to have Merge Replication in place, which includes having different database servers in different countries, entering data at their local times, and then the servers getting merged with the central server. Now let's look at how this concept of Merge Replication, proposed by Mr. Young, can be useful to us.

In this chapter, we will learn about Merge Replication and how to optimally configure it to gain the best performance out of it. We will also see how to troubleshoot common Merge Replication issues. The following are points we will cover in this chapter:

- Prerequisite and consideration before implementing Merge Replication
- A step-by-step installation of Merge Replication
- Configuration of Merge Replication using T-SQL

Merge Replication usages

Merge Replication is the most complex topology among all of the available replication types. When I speak about complexity, I refer to manageability. Managing Merge Replication is complex, as compared to other replication topologies.

Just like Transactional Replication, it starts with the snapshot of the publication database object and data, and then with the help of triggers, it keeps tracks of the data that is exchanged between Publisher and Subscriber. Once it has the changes available, it will synch the database at both the ends. With Merge Replication, we can allow various and/or physically dispersed locations to update, insert, or delete the data. Also, because the same operation can happen from more than one location, it is possible that a conflict may occur, which is resolved according to the standard conflict resolution method.

Typically, Merge Replication is suitable in the following scenarios:

* Multiple subscribers might update the same data at various times and propagate those changes to the Publisher and to other Subscribers
* There are chances of conflict, and so, there should be a mechanism to resolve it
* One-time modification is done from the Subscriber's end and should be updated at the Publisher's as well as the other Subscriber's end

How Merge Replication works

The following step-by-step process explains working of Merge Replication:

1. Data gets added from the Publisher's or the Subscriber's end.
2. The tracking table tracks the data that has been changed.
3. Merge Agent sends this data to the distribution database.
4. The distribution database sends this data back to the Merge Agent.
5. Merge Agent then sends this data to the Publisher and Subscriber(s).

Prerequisites for Merge Replication

As Merge Replication is the complex type of replication in terms of manageability, there are some points to be considered before we start with the installation of Merge Replication.

* **Unique identifier column:** There should be a **Globally Unique Identifier (GUID)** column in every table that is to be published. If this column does not exist, it will get added by Merge Replication process; Merge Replication will also create a unique index on this column.

- **Timestamp columns:** We should be extremely careful when replicating database(s) using Merge Replication, and especially with the Timestamp columns. Timestamp columns are supported, but the values of Timestamp will get regenerated when the snapshot is applied at the Subscriber end. Therefore, Timestamp columns are filtered when replication performs data validation.

- **Large Object (LOB) data types:** LOBs should be taken care of. We should set the value as `true` for the `@stream_blob_columns` of `sp_addmergearticle` parameter if there are LOB data types to publish. If we don't set the parameter value to `true`, the LOB should be in memory at the Publisher end, which will cause memory issues for the Publisher.

> If there are text, ntext, or image columns that are replicated, we should always use update statements right after the `updatetext` or `writetext` statement, so that it will fire trigger to update the metadata and make sure that the changes are propagated. It is recommended to use `varchar(max)`, `nvarchar(max)`, or `varbinary(max)` as data types instead of `text`, `ntext`, or `image`.

- **Bulk insertion:** When we insert data in bulk using BCP utility or bulk insert command, triggers will not get fired and the changes (insertion of data) will not be propagated to other nodes. In this case, any of the following methods should be followed:

  - Use `fire_triggers` option for bulk insert or with bcp utility. The syntax is:

    ```
    bcp AdventureWorks2008R2.Sales.Currency2 in Currency.dat -T
    -c -h "fire_triggers"
    Or
    BULKINSERT bulktest..t_float
    FROM'C:\t_float-c.dat'
    WITH
    (
    FORMATFILE='C:\t_floatformat-c-xml.xml',
    FIRE_TRIGGERS
    )
    GO
    ```

  - Execute `sp_addtablecontents` once we finish bcp or bulk insert. This procedure inserts references to the system tables. This helps keep data consistent across nodes. The following is the syntax:

    ```
    Sp_addtablecontents @table_name ='t_float'
    ```

- **Reference Table:** All referenced tables should be added so that the data consistency can be maintained.

- **"Not for Replication" property for identity columns and triggers**: Try to avoid using identity column as the primary key. But if it is already implemented, modify the property of the identity column as **Not For Replication**.

  Similarly, if we have triggers, add a line **Not For Replication** so that the trigger won't get fired when replication synchronizes data. If we do not mention this line in the trigger code, we might have inconsistent data. Refer to the sample code to know where to add this line:

```
CREATETRIGGER trg_testTrigger
ON tbl_TestTbl
AFTERINSERT,UPDATE
NotForReplication - Add this line before As
ASRAISERROR('Notify', 16, 10)
GO
```

Apart from the prerequisites/considerations listed here, there are some points that are already covered in the prerequisite section of the previous chapter. Let's have a line or two for the reference here.

- **Primary Key**: Every table should have a primary key to be the candidate table for Snapshot Replication.

- **Securing snapshot folder**: This is about the securing and accessing snapshot folder; please refer to the *Prerequisites for Snapshot replication* section in *Chapter 3, Snapshot Replication*, for more details.

- **Schedule**: This is about scheduling agent and jobs; refer to the *Prerequisites for Snapshot replication* section in Chapter 3 for more details.

- **Network bandwidth**: It talks about network bandwidth, which has already been discussed in the *Prerequisites...* section of Chapter 3.

- **Enough disk space for published database**: Please refer to the prerequisite section of *Chapter 4, Transactional Replication* for more details.

- **Enough disk space for distribution database**: Please refer to the prerequisite section of Chapter 4 for more details.

- **Domain account as service account**: Please refer to the prerequisite section of Chapter 4 for more details.

Installing Merge Replication

Let's now move ahead with the installation of Merge Replication. We have divided this into two parts—creating publication and creating subscription—to make it easy to understand.

Creating publication

1. Connect to the server we wish to act as a publisher. Expand the server and expand the replication node. Right-click on the **Publication** and select **New Publication**.

 We have a distributor created already; hence I am skipping that step here.

2. On the **Publication Database** wizard screen, select the database that we wish to publish and click **Next**.

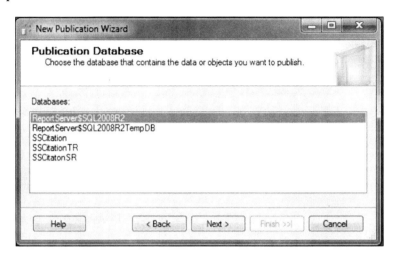

3. On the **Publication Type** screen, select the **Merge publication** option and click on the **Next** button.

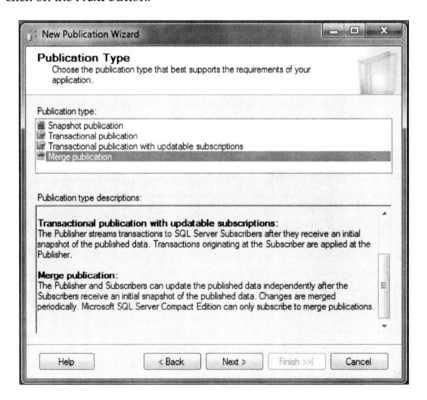

4. In the **Subscriber Types** screen, select the versions that we wish to act as subscribers and click **Next**.

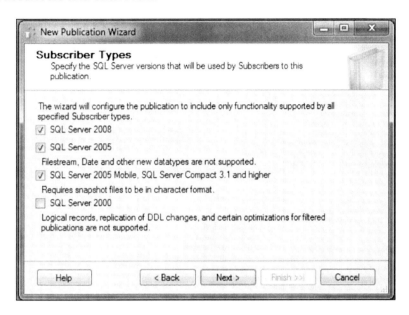

 SQL Server 2005 doesn't support `FileStream`, `Date`, and other new data types that are included in SQL Server 2008 R2.

5. In the **Articles** dialog box, select the articles to be published and click **Next**.

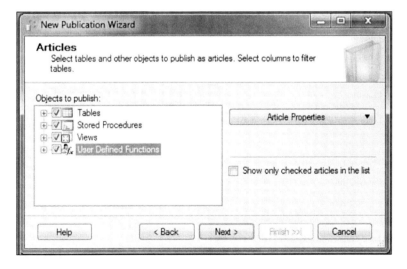

6. In the **Article Issues** dialog box, we are told about the changes we can make to our application, so that it keeps working as it was working prior to implementing Merge Replication.

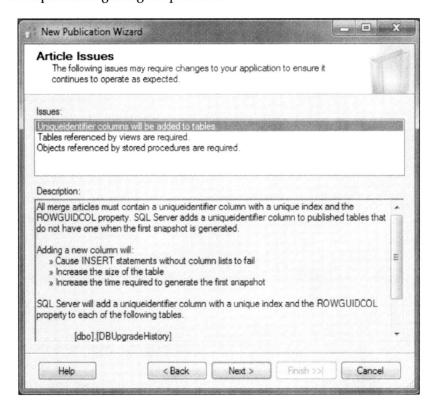

 Merge Replication will add the UniqueIdentifier column and a unique index in every table if they don't already exist. Tables that are referenced by views should be added for publication. Also, every object that is referenced by stored procedures (SPs) is required in publication.

7. In the filter table rows, add the filter (if required) based on the application/business logic and click **Next**.

8. In the **Snapshot Agent** dialog box, check the **Create a snapshot immediately** option to apply it to the Subscriber, check the **Schedule the Snapshot Agent to run...** option, and change the timing according to the business logic.

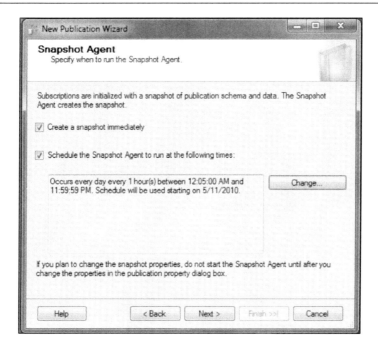

 Choose the time based on the allowed latency and size of the snapshot. A large number of articles as well as articles of a larger size will take longer to replicate.

9. In the **Agent Security** dialog box, click on security settings and specify the account under which to run the Snapshot Agent.

10. On the **Wizard Actions** screen, check **Create the publication** and **Generate a script file with steps to create the publication**, and click **Next**.

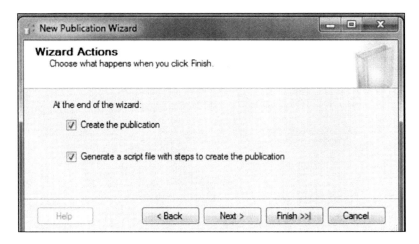

11. In the script file properties dialog box, specify the filename and file format, and click **Next**.

12. In the **Creating Publication** dialog box, verify that it shows a success report.

Creating subscription

As we have created a publication, let's now create a subscription. The following are the steps we need to follow:

1. Connect to the server we wish to act as a Subscriber and expand the server node and then the replication node. Right-click on the subscription node and select **New subscription**; this will bring the dialog box shown in the following screenshot:

2. In the **Publication** dialog box, select the Publisher from the drop-down box, and then select the database and the name of the publication we wish to use for the Subscriber we are creating here.

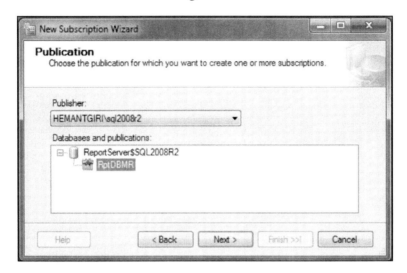

3. Select the location for Merge Agent to run either at **Distributor** or at **Subscriber** in the **Merge Agent Location** dialog box. Click **Next**.

4. Select the Subscribers and subscription database in the **Subscribers** dialog box and click **Next**.

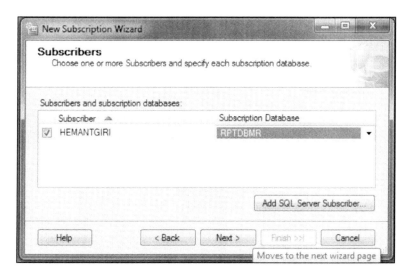

5. Select the account to select the agent, the account to run Merge Agent to connect to the Publisher and the Subscriber, and click **Next**.

6. In the **Initialize Subscriptions** dialog box, check whether to initialize subscription (**Initialize** checkbox) and when to initialize the subscription (**Initialize When** drop-down list) and click **Next**.

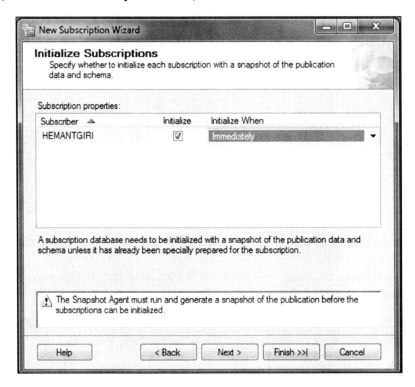

7. Select whether we need to have web synchronization (**Use Web Synchronization** checkbox). This feature is useful for synchronizing data using the HTTP protocol over the Internet, and it uses SSL to make data transmission secure. There are two components that will be used if we opt for web synchronization. They are as follows:

   ° `Replisapi.dll`: This acts as the listener that is configured on the IIS and will handle messages that are sent to the server from the publisher to subscribers.

   ° `Replrec.dll`: It is a reconciler that handles the XML data stream on each node.

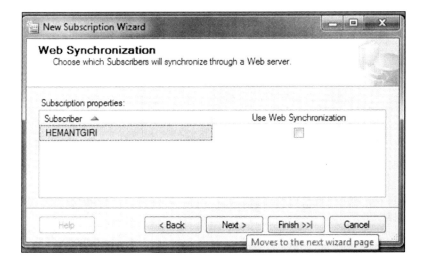

 Refer to the link mentioned in the External Reference section for further reading on web synchronization.

8. As shown in the following screenshot, we have selected **Server** as **Subscription Type**. We have set **75.00** as the value for **Priority for Conflict Resolution**. This means, in the case of conflict, in the Server subscription type, subscription priority is stored in the metadata for the change and merges the changes at other Subscribers.

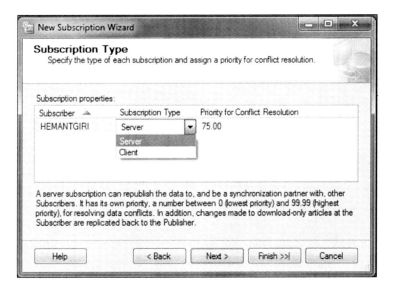

When we select Server as the subscription type, different Subscribers have different priorities and this cannot be assigned explicitly. But this can be decided based on whether it is republishing the database; hence, the top-level publisher will have 100.00 as the priority whereas others will have values less than 100.00.

With Client as the subscription type, all subscriptions have the same priority and the first subscriber will win the conflict.

9. Check the **Creating subscription...** and **Generating a script file** options and click **Next**.

10. In the script file properties dialog box, specify the filename and file format and click **Next**.

11. In the **Creating Subscription(s)...** step, verify that the result pane shows the success report.

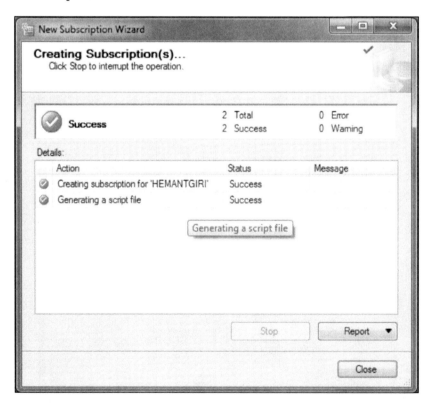

Configuration

We have installed Merge Replication using GUI; let's now learn to install Merge Replication using T-SQL.

Configuring publication using T-SQL

The first step is to create a Distributor. As we have already created a Distributor, we will create publication. We need to execute the following T-SQL to create publication:

```
-- This will enable database for Replication
use [ReportServer$SQL2008R2]
execsp_replicationdboption
@dbname =N'ReportServer$SQL2008R2',
@optname =N'merge publish',
@value =N'true'
GO
/*
Please notice that to add publication with Merge replication we have
to use sp_addMERGEpublication, unlike snapshot
and transaction replication where we are using sp_addpublication
*/

use [ReportServer$SQL2008R2]
execsp_addmergepublication@publication =N'RptDBMR',
@description =N'Merge publication of database ''ReportServer$SQL2008R2
'' from Publisher ''HEMANTGIRI\SQL2008R2''.',
@sync_mode =N'character',
@retention = 14,
@allow_push =N'true',
@allow_pull =N'true',
@allow_anonymous =N'true',
@enabled_for_internet =N'false',
@snapshot_in_defaultfolder =N'true',
@compress_snapshot =N'false',
@ftp_port = 21,
@ftp_subdirectory =N'ftp',
@ftp_login =N'anonymous',
@allow_subscription_copy =N'false',
@add_to_active_directory =N'false',
@dynamic_filters =N'false',
@conflict_retention = 14,
@keep_partition_changes =N'false',
@allow_synctoalternate =N'false',
```

```
@max_concurrent_merge = 0,
@max_concurrent_dynamic_snapshots = 0,
@use_partition_groups =null,
/*
Recall that we have selected SQL Server version 2005 and above for
subscriber type
and hence compatibility level is 90RTM, that means newly added
datatype i.e. date and
FileStream are not supported if subscriber is on SQL Server 2005
*/
@publication_compatibility_level =N'90RTM',
@replicate_ddl = 1,
@allow_subscriber_initiated_snapshot =N'false',
@allow_web_synchronization =N'true',
@allow_partition_realignment =N'true',
@retention_period_unit =N'days',
@conflict_logging =N'both',
@automatic_reinitialization_policy = 0
GO


-- This will add publication snapshot
execsp_addpublication_snapshot
@publication =N'RptDBMR',
@frequency_type = 4,
@frequency_interval = 1,
@frequency_relative_interval = 1,
@frequency_recurrence_factor = 0,
@frequency_subday = 8,
@frequency_subday_interval = 1,
@active_start_time_of_day = 500,
@active_end_time_of_day = 235959,
@active_start_date = 0,
@active_end_date = 0,
@job_login =null,
@job_password =null,
@publisher_security_mode = 1


/*
To add an article there is a different stored procedure in merge
replication
sp_addmergearticle, if we need to drop an article we should use sp_
dropmergearticle
*/
use [ReportServer$SQL2008R2]
execsp_addmergearticle
```

```
@publication =N'RptDBMR',
@article =N'ActiveSubscriptions',
@source_owner =N'dbo',
@source_object =N'ActiveSubscriptions',
@type =N'table',
@description =null,
@creation_script =null,
@pre_creation_cmd =N'drop',
@schema_option = 0x000000B208034FF1,
@identityrangemanagementoption =N'manual',
@force_reinit_subscription = 1,
@column_tracking =N'false',
@subset_filterclause =null,
@vertical_partition =N'false',
@verify_resolver_signature = 1,
@allow_interactive_resolver =N'false',
@fast_multicol_updateproc =N'true',
@check_permissions = 0,
@subscriber_upload_options = 0,
@delete_tracking =N'true',
@compensate_for_errors =N'false',
@stream_blob_columns =N'false',
@partition_options = 0
GO
```

Configuring the Subscriber using T-SQL

The second step is to create a Subscriber. This can be achieved by executing the
following T-SQL code:

```
----------------BEGIN: Script to be run at Publisher
use [ReportServer$SQL2008R2]
execsp_addmergesubscription
@publication =N'RptDBMR',
@subscriber =N'HEMANTGIRI',
@subscriber_db =N'RPTDBMR',
@subscription_type =N'pull',
@subscriber_type =N'global',
@subscription_priority = 75,
@sync_type =N'Automatic'
GO
----------------END: Script to be run at Publisher
----------------BEGIN: Script to be run at Subscriber
use [RPTDBMR]
```

```
execsp_addmergepullsubscription
-- Name of the publisher
@publisher =N'HEMANTGIRI\SQL2008R2',
-- Name of the publication
@publication =N'RptDBMR',
-- database which will get published
@publisher_db =N'ReportServer$SQL2008R2',
-- Is subscriber known to all server or to publisher only?
@subscriber_type =N'Global',
-- This number indicates the priority for subscription
@subscription_priority = 75,
@description =N'',
@sync_type =N'Automatic'
execsp_addmergepullsubscription_agent
@publisher =N'HEMANTGIRI\SQL2008R2',
@publisher_db =N'ReportServer$SQL2008R2',
@publication =N'RptDBMR',
@distributor =N'HEMANTGIRI\SQL2008R2',
@distributor_security_mode = 1,
@distributor_login =N'',
@distributor_password =null,
@enabled_for_syncmgr =N'False',
@frequency_type = 64,
@frequency_interval = 0,
@frequency_relative_interval = 0,
@frequency_recurrence_factor = 0,
@frequency_subday = 0,
@frequency_subday_interval = 0,
@active_start_time_of_day = 0,
@active_end_time_of_day = 235959,
@active_start_date = 20100511,
@active_end_date = 99991231,
@alt_snapshot_folder =N'',
@working_directory =N'',
@use_ftp =N'False',
@job_login =null,
@job_password =null,
@publisher_security_mode = 1,
@publisher_login =null,
@publisher_password =null,
@use_interactive_resolver =N'False',
@dynamic_snapshot_location =null,
-- Is this enable for web synchronization?
@use_web_sync = 0
GO
----------------END: Script to be run at Subscriber
```

Creating alternate synchronization partner using T-SQL

What will happen if something goes wrong with the Publisher? Microsoft SQL Server will allow us to create an alternate synchronization partner that can take over control as a Publisher if our main Publisher goes down for any reason. To create an alternate Publisher, we have to execute the following T-SQL code on the server that we wish to create as a synchronization partner:

```
use [dbname]
go
sp_addmergealternatepublisher
-- This will be the name of the publisher
@publisher ='publisher',
-- The publication database
@publisher_db ='publisher_db',
-- Publication name
@publication ='publication',
-- Alternate Publisher name
@alternate_publisher ='alternate_synchronization_partner',
-- Alternate publication database name
@alternate_publisher_db ='alternate_publisher_db',
-- alternate publication name
@alternate_publication ='alternate_synchronization_partner',
-- alternate distributor if any
@alternate_distributor ='alternate_distributor',
-- Friendly name used to identified alternate synchronization partner
by publisher, publication and distributor
@friendly_name ='friendly_name'
```

Note: Only those users who are members of the sysadmin fixed server role, or db_owner fixed db role, can execute the `sp_addmergealternatepublisher` system stored procedure.

Dropping an alternate synchronization partner using T-SQL

The following code will drop an alternate synchronization partner.

 Note: Only the sysadmin fixed server role or db_owner fixed db role can execute sp_addmergealternatepublisher.

```
/* This will drop alternate synchronization partner
Note: Only sysadmin fixed server role or db_owner fixed db role can
execute
sp_addmergealternatepublisher
*/
use [dbname]
go
sp_dropmergealternatepublisher
-- This will be the name of the publisher
@publisher ='publisher',
-- The publication database
@publisher_db ='publisher_db',
-- Publication name
@publication ='publication',
-- Alternate Publisher name
@alternate_publisher ='alternate_synchronization_partner',
-- Alternate publication database name
@alternate_publisher_db ='alternate_publisher_db',
-- alternate publication name
@alternate_publication ='alternate_synchronization_partner'
```

Uninstalling subscription

In any case, if we need to remove subscription, we shall execute the following T-SQL batch:

```
/* Execute this batch the Subscriber end to remove a merge pull
subscription.
 */
USE [AdventureWorksReplica]
EXECsp_dropmergepullsubscription
@publisher = @publisher,
  @publisher_db = @publication_db,
  @publication = @publication;
GO
```

```
/*
Execute this batch at the Publisher end to remove a pull or push
subscription to a merge publication.
*/
USE [AdventureWorks]
EXECsp_dropmergesubscription
@publication = @publication,
  @subscriber = @subscriber,
  @subscriber_db = @subscriptionDB;
GO
```

Configuring download-only articles

Download-only articles are those articles that cannot be updated—no insertions, updates, or deletions can take place at the Subscriber end. This is beneficial when a product's master needs to be updated and usually happens at the Publisher end, that is, Jewellery Master.

The advantage of this will be seen in relation to the network. As this is a download-only article, there will be one-way traffic for this article and hence network consumption can be reduced. We may observe a significant performance boost with this.

There are two ways of defining an article as a download-only article—using SSMS and T-SQL.

- **Using SSMS**:

   Follow the steps given next:

   1. Connect to the Publisher server.
   2. Expand the Replication Node.
   3. Expand the Publication Node.
   4. Right-click on the publication name and select **Properties**.
   5. Select **Article Properties**.
   6. Select a table.
   7. Click on the set properties of the highlighted table article.
   8. Under **Properties** tab in the destination object selection, change the value of **Synchronization direction** to any of the following: **Download to Subscriber, prohibit Subscriber changes** or **Download to Subscriber, allow Subscriber changes**.
   9. Click **OK**.

- **Using T-SQL**:

  Follow the steps given next:

  1. Execute `sp_helpmergearticle 'articlename'` and note down the value of `upload_options`.

  2. If it returns `0`, then execute the following T-SQL:

```
/*
after executing sp_helpmergearticle note down the value
for upload_options
*/
sp_helpmergearticle
@publication='ThreadSmith_SQL_ReplPub',
@article='order'
go
/*
If the value returned is 0, execute below T-SQL code.
@Property specify which property requires value to be
changed, and
@value specifies what value it should have. @force_
invalidate_snapshot=1
will make snapshot to be invalidate and @force_reinit_
subscription=1 will
reinitialize the subscription next time agent will run. @
value can have either 1 or 2 where:
1 = Changes are allowed at the subscriber, but they are not
uploaded to the publisher
2 = Changes are not allowed at the subscriber
*/
sp_changemergearticle
@publication='ThreadSmith_SQL_ReplPub',
@article='order',
@property=Subscriber_upload_options
@value=1
@force_invalidate_snapshot=1
@force_reinit_subscription=1
```

 If the source table is a part of more than one publication, the value for the `Subscriber_upload_options` property should be similar in every publication.

Configuring alerts using SSMS

Here are the steps we need to follow while configuring alerts using SSMS:

1. Launch the Replication Monitor by right-clicking on the Replication Node or by calling `sqlmonitor.exe`.

2. Right-click on the publication and select **Configure Replication Alert**, similar to one we can see in the following screenshot:

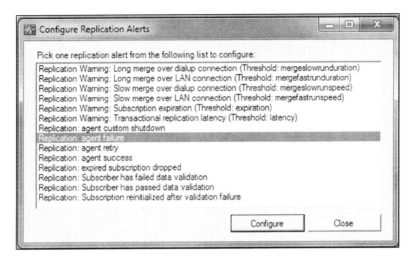

3. Select any of the alerts and click **Configure**.

4. In the general section, name the Replication Agent, and select the appropriate type and database name.

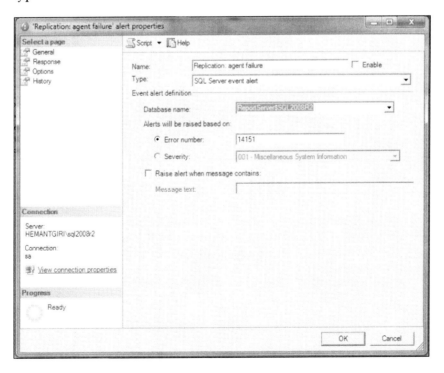

5. Click on the **Response** option in the left pane. In the right pane, click **Notify operators** to decide to whom to send the alerts.

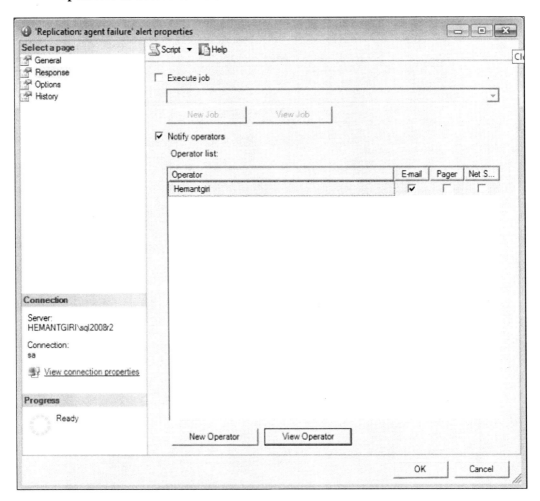

I have already configured the operator and database mail on my server. Here is the link to a nice article on how to configure the database mail functionality: http://www.sql-server-performance.com/ articles/dba/email_functionality_p1.aspx. This article is for SQL Server 2005, but the steps will be the same for SQL Server 2008.

6. Click **View Operator**. In the left pane, click **Notifications** and select the alert name we wish to configure e-mails for.

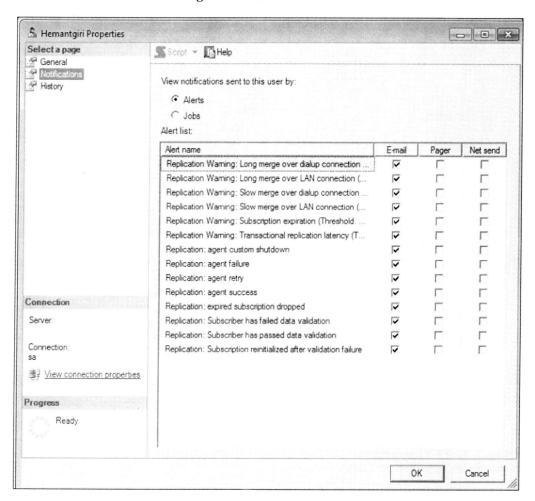

Click **OK** and close the dialog box. This way, we can configure the alert, so that whenever anything goes wrong with the replication, we will receive an e-mail alert.

The following screenshot shows an example of such an alert:

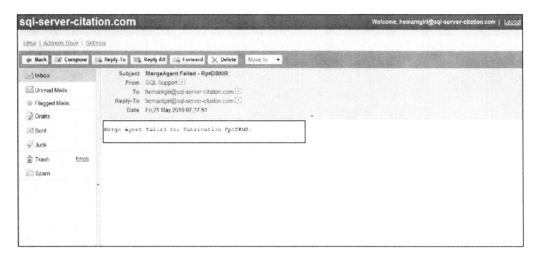

 This can also be achieved by adding an additional step to send an e-mail in to the replication jobs created by the Replication wizard.

Summary

In this chapter, we learned what Merge Replication is, how it works, what are the prerequisites, and how to configure Merge Replication using T-SQL as well as using a wizard from SQL Server Management Studio. We have also explored the possible areas wherein we can implement Merge Replication. In the next chapter, we will learn about Peer-to-Peer Replication.

6
Peer-to-Peer Replication

Mr. Young is a DBA with XY Incorporation. The company has a data center located in the main campus and has recently developed a homegrown ERP system that is hosted on the SQL Server Database. This application will be the main production application, and thus the application and the database is very critical to the company. While the development team was estimating the future growth of the database, they took the help of Mr. Young. According to Mr. Young, it would grow 40 GB per year and they would be exposing some part of the data to the external users for reporting.

During the board meeting, management had asked Mr. Young to design an infrastructure that can handle the load in the early stage of the application as well as in the future. Also, the database should be highly available to the internal and external users with minimal downtime. After a few days of research, Mr. Young finally prepared a plan to implement the Peer-to-Peer (P2P) Replication, so that he can make use of existing SQL Servers for load balancing and make the database highly available in case of any emergency. Because he is installing P2P replication for the first time, let's help him by sharing notes with him.

In the previous chapter, we learned how to install, configure, and troubleshoot common errors of Merge Replication. In this chapter, we will learn about Peer-to-Peer (P2P) Replication and how it works. We will also see:

- The prerequisites of Peer-to-Peer Replication
- How to install Peer-to-Peer Replication
- How to configure Peer-to-Peer Replication

What is Peer-to-Peer Replication?

Peer-to-Peer Replication type was introduced with the launch of SQL Server 2005, and is the most promising solution when the ultimate goal is to achieve data redundancy and load balancing. Peer-to-Peer Replication is built on top of the Transactional Replication type, where every participant node has a copy of the data, which results in the redundancy of data and ensures that we have high availability. Ultimately, we have achieved a higher response time while reading data from server, along with the high availability of data.

At the same time, we will also get the benefit of load balancing using the Peer-to-Peer Replication type. While configuring P2P replication, we can authorize or allocate the objects between participant nodes to achieve load balancing.

With P2P replications, we can be assured that if one node fails, P2P Replication is still able to work. This is because any of the participant nodes can act as a Publisher, and hence there is *no single point-of-failure*.

Let's now see how Peer-to-Peer Replication helps us achieve both performance boost and high availability.

How Peer-to-Peer Replication works

Let's look at a scenario with the help of the following diagram. P2P replication is configured on two servers—Server A and Server B. There are four, or more than four, workstations connected to the Application Server, which sends and receives data from the database servers (in this case, Server A and Server B).

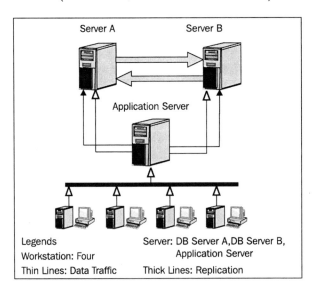

Now, Server A and Server B have replication set up, which has almost identical data spread between two of them. If we take a look, there are thick bi-directional lines that indicate the bi-directional data flow between Server A and Server B. On the other hand, the thin lines show the traffic routed from the Application Server to the Database Server. One line is used to read data that is spread between servers (SQL Server decides where to route traffic randomly for read operation), whereas for writing to the database, we can have our application with logic that assigns which objects will have write permission on which server—for example, tables starting with letter A to H should write/update data on Server A and tables starting with letter I to Z should write/update data on Server B. This ensures no update is lost as updates or insertions happen on different servers, based on the logic we have used to isolate the tables.

Prerequisites for Peer-to-Peer Replication

Let's now see the prerequisites for implementing the Peer-to-Peer Replication.

- **SQL Server Edition**: P2P Replication is available with the Enterprise Edition only.

- **Schema and Data**: All databases that participate in the P2P network should have identical schema and data. The names of objects should be identical. Ensure that the publication allows schema changes to replicate.

- **Filtering**: Ensure that we don't have row and column filtering as P2P Replication doesn't support row-and column-level filtering.

- **Primary Key**: It is a basic rule that every table should have a Primary Key to be a candidate table for Transactional Replication.

- **Securing snapshot folder**: This is about securing and accessing the snapshot folder. Please refer to the prerequisite section of Snapshot Replication (Chapter 3) for more details.

- **Schedule**: This is about scheduling the agent and jobs. Please refer to the prerequisite section of Snapshot Replication (Chapter 3) for more details.

- **Network bandwidth**: Network bandwidth has been discussed in the prerequisite section of Snapshot Replication (Chapter 3).

- **Enough disk space for the database that is being published**: We need to make sure that we have ample space available for the transaction log of the published database, as it will continue to grow and won't truncate the log records until they are moved to a distribution database. Hence, it is recommended to set t-log's auto grow option to the value true. We should also make sure that the distribution database is available and the log reader agent is running.

- **Enough disk space for the distribution database**: It is necessary to have enough disk space allocated for the distribution database. This is because it will store the transactions marked for replication until it is applied to the subscriber database within the limit of the retention period of distribution (by default, 72 hours), or it will keep the transaction until the snapshot agent re-runs and creates a new snapshot. Hence, to store the transactions that are marked for replication, we should have enough disk space available for the distribution database.

- **Use the domain account as a service account**: We should always use the domain account as a service account, so that when agents access the shared folder of snapshot files, they won't have any problem just because they are local to the system and do not have permission to access network share. While mentioning the service account, we are asked to choose from two built-in accounts including a Local System account and Network Services, and a box captioned this account wherein we have to specify the domain account on which the service account will run.

Installing Peer-to-Peer Replication

As we discussed earlier, P2P is built on top of Transactional Replication and we will have to install Transactional Replication before we go about installing P2P Replication. It is about changing the properties in Publication, and hence we will skip most of the snapshots that will get repeated here. Let's start installing Transactional Replication by creating a new publication.

As P2P is a subtype of Transactional Replication, the initial steps in the installation are similar, and so we will cover only those steps that are different. To know about the initial common steps in installation, refer to the steps under the *Creating new publication for Transactional Replication* and the *Creating subscription for Transactional Replication* sections in *Chapter 4, Transactional Replication*. Let's start.

1. Once we configure Transactional Replication, we will be able to start configuring P2P Replication. Right-click on the **Publication** and select **Properties**.

2. Select the **Subscription** page.

3. On the **Subscription** page, set the **Allow Peer-to-Peer subscriptions** option to **True** in the Peer-to-Peer properties.

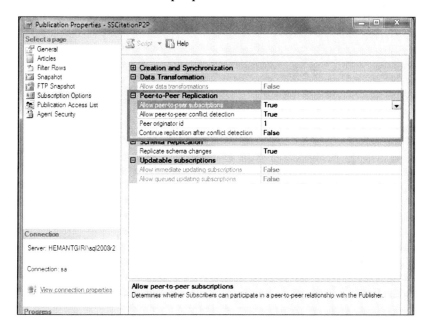

 Please note that SQL Server 2008 R2 supports the conflict detection method. If we want our setup to detect conflicts, we have to set the **Allow peer-to-peer conflict detection** option to **True,** as shown in the preceding screenshot.

4. Once we have enabled the P2P subscription, right-click on the **Publisher** and we will be able to see the new context menu option named **Configure Peer-to-Peer topology...**. Click on that option.

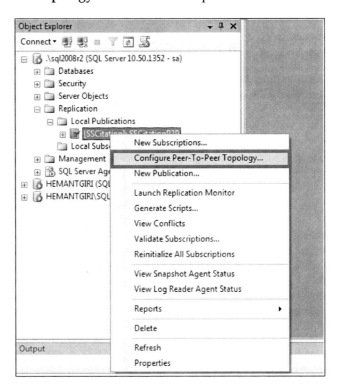

5. At this point, select the database and publication and click **Next**.

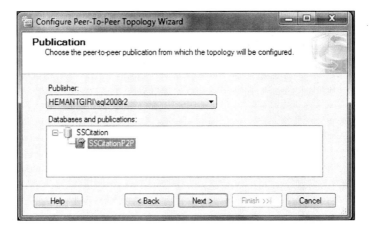

6. In the **Configure Topology** dialog box, click the **Add a New Peer Node** option.

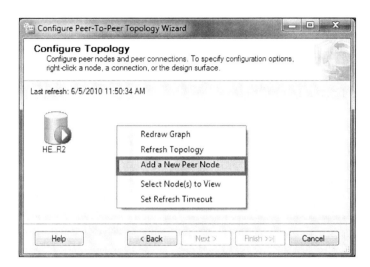

7. We will be asked to connect to the server that we want to add as a node in the P2P replication topology.

8. In the **Add a New Peer Node** section, select the database name and specify the **Peer Originator ID**. We need to make sure that the Peer Originator ID is unique.

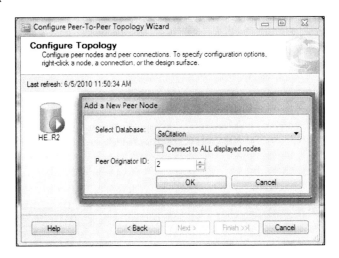

9. In the next screen, specify the connection option for the Log Reader Agent and click **Next**.

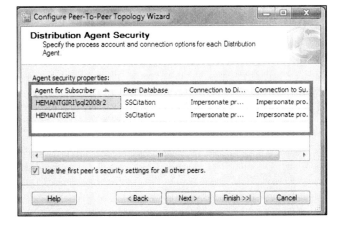

10. In the **New Peer Initialization** box, choose the appropriate option. If we have created the peer database including schema and data, either using backup or scripting and SSIS, select the first option. In case there is a modification in the published database, we should restore the latest publication database. To do this, select the second option and specify the backup file and backup file location.

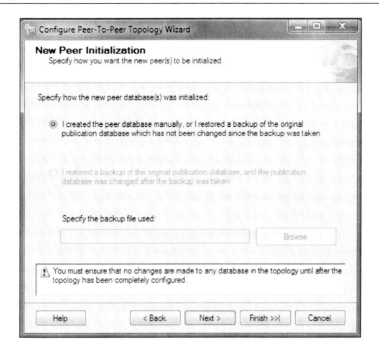

11. In the **Complete the Wizard** dialog, verify the information we have provided until now and click **Finish**.

12. In the final screen, confirm that every step we perform returns the successful status.

Configuration

In this section, we will learn how to configure alerts for Peer-to-Peer Replication. We will also learn how to remove a Peer Node and will add a new SQL Server 2005 instance as a new node. Because SQL Server 2005 doesn't support conflict detection, we have to disable conflict detection in the publication properties before adding SQL Server 2005 as a node.

Configuring alerts

So far we have learned how to install P2P Replication; let's now learn how to configure the alerts for the errors or conflicts, that is, conflict detection.

1. Right-click on the `Replication` folder and select **Launch Replication Monitor**, or call `sqlmonitor.exe` to launch the replication monitor.

2. In the warning tab, click on the **Configure Alerts** button; this will bring up the screen shown here:

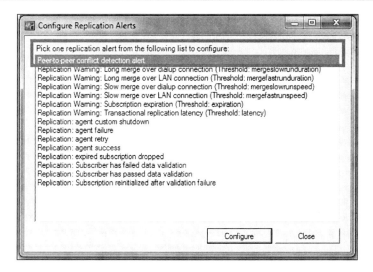

3. In the properties screen, check the box next to the **Peer-to-Peer conflict detection alert** option and click **Configure**.

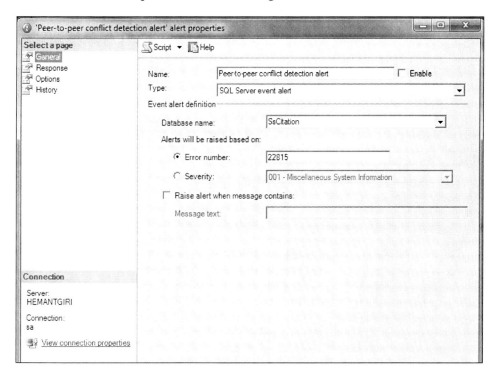

4. In the **Response** tab, check the **Notify operators** option, and from there, select any one of the **E-mail**, **Pager**, or **Net Send** options to notify in case something goes wrong with the replication.

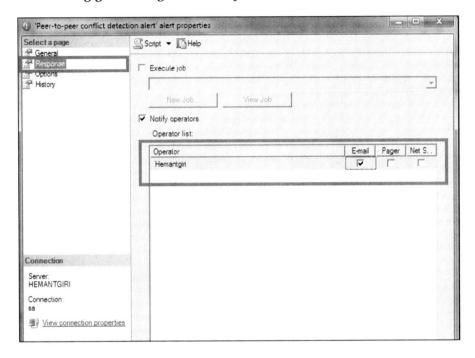

Removing a node from Peer-to-Peer Replication

In any case, if we need to remove a node from the P2P Replication, here are the steps that we need to follow:

1. Connect to the server and expand the replication node.

2. Select **Configure Peer-to-Peer Topology…**.

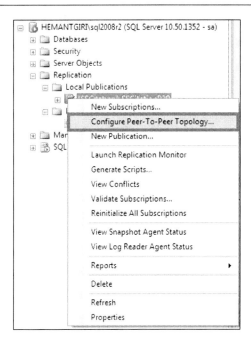

3. Select publication and database and click **Next**.

4. Select the **Delete Peer Node** option.

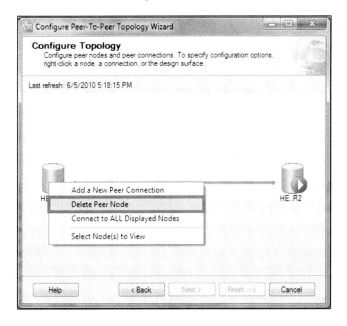

5. In the **Configure Topology** screen, select the node we want to delete and confirm the action by clicking **OK**.

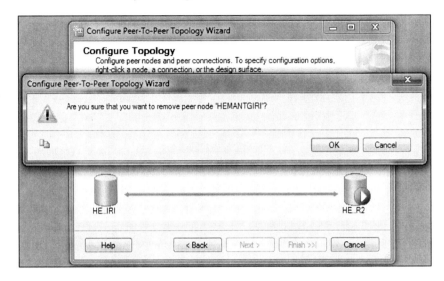

6. In the **Complete the Wizard** dialog box, verify the action. This will delete the subscription and publication on server **Hemantgiri**, because we are deleting **Hemantgiri** as a node from Peer-to-Peer Replication.

7. As soon as we click **Finish**, it will start deleting subscriptions and publication. We need to ensure that we get a success message at the end.

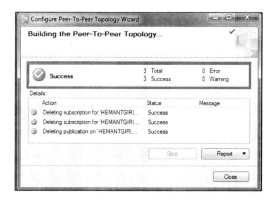

Adding SQL Server 2005 as a Peer-to-Peer node

If, for some reasons, we need to add SQL Server 2005 as a P2P Node, here are the steps to follow:

1. As SQL Server 2005 doesn't support conflict detection for P2P Replication, we have to disable the conflict detection, as shown in the following screenshot, before we go about adding a SQL Server 2005 as a new Peer-to-Peer node.

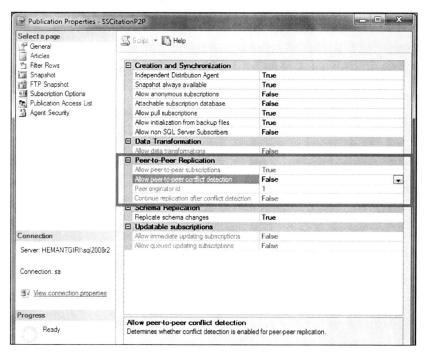

2. Expand the replication node. Select **Configure Peer-to-Peer Replication**.

3. Select the publication and database.

4. In the **Configure Topology** screen, right-click and select **Add a New Peer Node**.

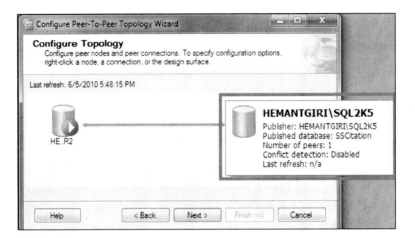

 Notice that this is the SQL Server 2005 instance and that the conflict detection has been disabled.

5. Specify the **Log Reader Agent Security** account details and click **Next**.

6. In the **Distribution Agent Security** screen, specify the accounts for the distribution agent and click **Next**.

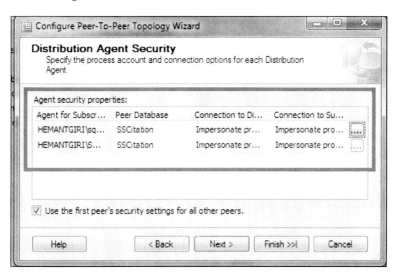

7. In the **New Peer Initialization** screen, select the first option. As we cannot restore the database using a backup file of SQL Server 2008 R2 to SQL Server 2005, I created an empty database and then copied the schema and data using SSIS.

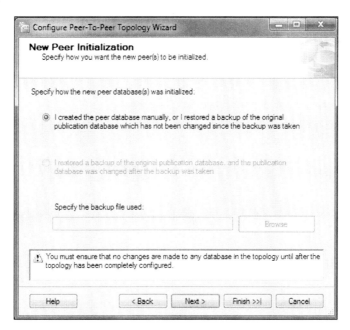

8. In the **Complete the Wizard** section, verify the options we have specified and click **Finish**. This will add the SQL Server 2005 as a Peer-to-Peer node.

Summary

In this chapter, we learned how to install P2P Replication using a wizard, as well as how to configure P2P Replication to drop a node. We looked at how to add a SQL Server 2005 node to P2P topology in the existing setup. We also covered the conflict detection method and how to create alerts if a conflict or error occurs.

In the next chapter, we will learn about Log Shipping.

7
Log Shipping

Mr. Young is the System Administrator of XY Incorporation, which is a mid-size manufacturing company. He is responsible for maintaining the overall IT Infrastructure of this company. Mr. Young has configured the database server properly and has a good backup strategy on which he and his company rely in case of any emergency. This database server hosts our company's (XY Incorporation) mission-critical databases. We were very happy with the setup, until one fine day, when the database server crashed.

It was an outage of around 45 minutes. By the time the full database backup and subsequent transaction log files were restored, and applications were made to point to the new database server, the company had incurred a loss of thousands of rupees and its reputation was at stake. A meeting was called by the board of directors, where Mr. Young was asked to configure the database server in such a way that it can be made available in approximately two to 10 minutes in such a scenario, and it should be cheaper, easy to manage, and needs minimal human intervention. After careful analysis, Mr. Young presented his report to the directors, suggesting that it is better to implement Log Shipping, as it is cheaper, easy to manage, and will also use the existing backup strategy that the company has.

Once Log Shipping was implemented, Mr. Young observed that it really worked well and is easy to manage. To test the role switch or failover during a planned maintenance window, Mr. Young performed a sample test and the secondary database server was up within five minutes, which is the desired output.

From the previous example, we've seen that it is really nice to have some High Availability system to be configured based on the requirement and our environment. Let's have a look at the significance of configuring Log Shipping, and how to install and troubleshoot it.

In this chapter, we will learn:

- What is Log Shipping
- Why and in what condition should Log Shipping be implemented
- What are the prerequisites of establishing Log Shipping, and how to establish it using T-SQL
- How to troubleshoot common issues

What is Log Shipping?

Log Shipping is one of the solutions that are available with SQL Server to cater to the needs of highly available business applications. It was first introduced with the release of SQL Server 7.0.

As its name suggests, it ships the transaction logs (T-Log) of the one server (primary) to another server (secondary) over the network, to keep the Secondary Server synchronized with the Primary Server. In case of the failure of the Primary Server, we can quickly move over to Secondary Server with the help of just a few steps.

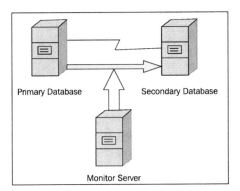

How Log Shipping works

As of now, we have understood what Log Shipping is and how it works. Now let's have a look at why we should have Log Shipping as a High Availability option or as a Disaster Recovery option in our environment. There are a few points I can pen down as a justification.

- **Easier to set up:** It's really an easy job to create Log Shipping. The only thing we need to identify is that we must have two or three servers. The witness server(first is primary/source server and second is secondary/target server) is optional to configure, and it is acceptable if this witness server is not identical to other machines.

- **Manageability:** Managing Log Shipping is the simplest among the available HA options that we have with SQL Server. There are only a few errors that can show up with the Log Shipping and they are quite simple to solve (we will see this in the appendix on troubleshooting in detail).

- **Can act as a Reporting server:** The Secondary or standby server can act as a Reporting server. We may use this server to read only queries, or to generate reports from. Although, it is really easy to get it working as a reporting server, we need to consider the latency. This means if the T-Log backup copy and restoration would take 10 minutes, and we have scheduled T-Log backup every hour, we will observe 10 minutes delay in data / per hour.

- **Multiple database(s)/servers:** We may use multiple servers as a standby/ Secondary Server, where one server can be used for reporting purposes, whereas the other can be utilized for HA only.

- **Cheaper than cluster:** If we go for clustering, we have to have a special hardware that is compatible with clustering and should be identical in all the participating nodes. On the contrary, Log Shipping doesn't require the same set of hardware.

Prerequisites for Log Shipping

Let's quickly go through the prerequisites for Log Shipping. They are as follows:

- **Recovery model:** We should make sure that the database on which we need to enable Log Shipping should be in either a Full or Bulk-Logged recovery model. Here is a table that will brief us about different recovery models and the type of recovery they can provide:

Recovery model	Benefit	Loss of data	Type of recovery
Simple	Keeps T-Log in small size, can perform bulk copy operation	If needed, we have to restore Full backup or Differential backup	Possible till the last backup time
Bulk-Logged	Minimal log space occupation, can perform bulk operation	If the log is damaged or bulk operation is done after last T-Log backup	Can be performed up till the last backup time
Full	No work lost due to damaged data file, point-in-time recovery	Normally none, only if we have lost our most recent T-Log backup	Point-in-time

- **Accounts:** We should make sure that the account that runs the log shipping jobs has SA rights on both the servers.

- **Share**: We need to make sure that the service account we are using has the read and write access permission on both the servers, for them to be able to copy and paste the T-Log backup without any issue.

- **Login sync:** This is not purely a point to be included here; however, this point is most essential—when we switch over the role in a Log Shipping, all the logins should be available at the secondary database as well. To synchronize the logins, we may use BCP command, SSIS, or the `sp_help_revlogin` stored procedure, and ensure that there are no orphaned users.

Installing Primary Server

The very first step is to enable the database for Log Shipping.

1. To do so, right-click on the database that we want to configure with Log Shipping and select **Ship Transaction Logs...** from the **Tasks** menu.

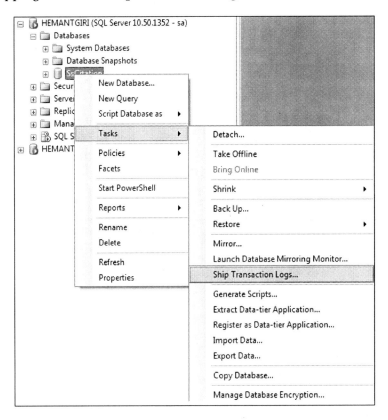

2. To enable the database for Log Shipping, click **Ship Transaction Logs...**and
   check the **Enable this as a primary database in a log shipping configuration**
   option. This will enable the database as shown in the following screenshot:

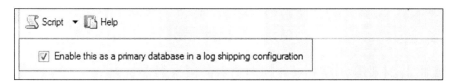

3. The next step is to configure the T-Log backup. We have kept the
   default schedule intact. Click on the **Backup Settings** option to
   configure backup options.

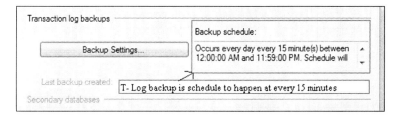

4. In the backup settings, mention the network path where we will keep the
   T-Log backup files. These files will then be copied over to the local folder of
   the Secondary Server somewhere (this can be configured using T-SQL, and
   we will see this later).

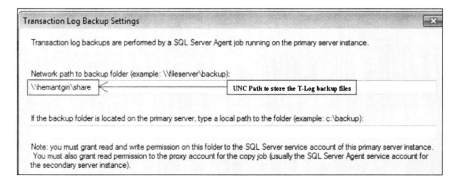

 As mentioned in the prerequisites, please assign read and
write permission to the service account on this folder.

5. Just below the **Network path to backup folder...** option, we can see the options to set values for backup file retention period (**72** hours by default). There is also a setting to send an alert if no backup takes place within the specified duration (**1** hour by default).

6. As we are done with the backup retention period and alert settings, let's configure the schedule for T-Log backup job. I have kept the default settings intact, but one may want to change the timings to some different values by clicking on the **Schedule...** button.

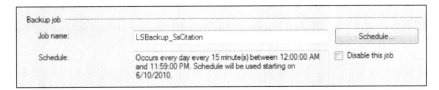

7. We have an option to compress the backup. SQL Server 2008 has a new feature called **backup and data compression**. This option reduces the size of the backup file, so that it gets transmitted quickly over the network.

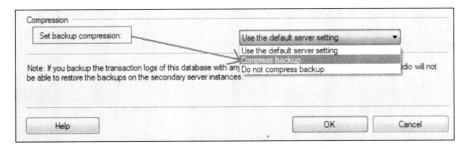

Setting up the secondary database

Now that we are done setting up the primary database, let's set up the secondary database and then specify where to copy files in order to finish the installation step.

1. Once we are done with the backup settings, we will notice that the **Add** button under the **Secondary Database** option is enabled. Clicking on the **Add** button will display the following screen:

In this screenshot, connect to the Secondary Server and choose the database we want to act as the secondary database. There are a few options on the **Initialize secondary database** tab; let's now see them one by one.

- ° **Yes, generate a full backup of the primary database and restore it into the secondary database…**:This option will take a full backup of the primary database and then restore it over the secondary database; the option will create the secondary database if it doesn't exist. Along with this, we may also specify the path for the data and log files by clicking on the **Restore Options…**button.

- Yes, restore an existing backup of the primary database into the secondary database...: This option will restore the database from the existing full backup stored on either network, or from the local path of the secondary database. Again, we have an option of specifying the path for the data and log files by clicking on the **Restore Options...** button.

- No, the secondary database is initialized: Select this option when the database on the Secondary Server has up-to-date schema and data, or latest backup has already been restored.

2. In the next tab, we will be configuring options such as where to keep the T-Log backup files on the destination server and what will be the retention period for it. We will also be scheduling the job for copying files.

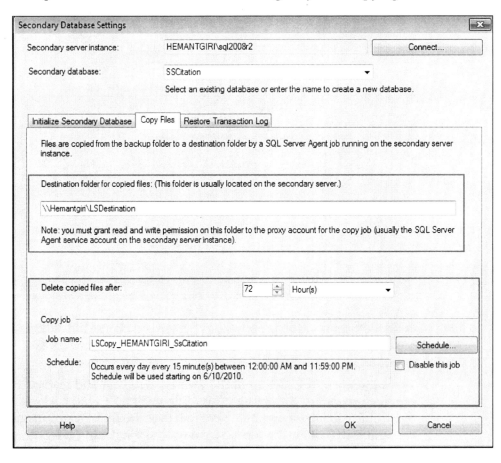

- The very first option is about specifying the shared location where we will be storing T-Log files on the Secondary Server. We should ensure that the agent service account under which the job is going to perform the restoration of T-Log file has the required permission, that is, Read and Write permission.

- We should mention the retention period for copied T-Log backup files according to business needs. Here, I have retained the default value of **72** hours as can be seen from the preceding screenshot.

- In the **Copy job** section, click on the **Schedule...** button and we will be able to change the frequency and daily frequency for the job to be executed.

3. The third tab of the **Secondary Database Settings** is about configuring the various options for restoring transaction log such as database state, delay restoration, alerts, and T-Log restoration job. Let's see these options one by one.

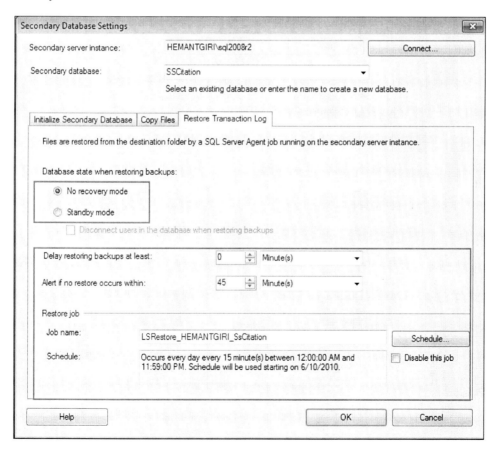

- ° **Database State...**: This is a very crucial point while configuring Log Shipping, as this will define whether or not the database on the Secondary Server is accessible for reporting/read-only purposes, depending on the database state we have defined. Let's get a better idea of what this means.

- ° **No recovery mode:** This option will tell the SQL Server Engine that the restoration is not yet over and there are subsequent backup files that are going to be applied here. While database is in **No recovery mode**, we are not allowed to make connections, which means we cannot use this database state if we want our secondary database to be used as a reporting/read-only instance.

- ° **Standby mode**: This option will tell SQL Server Engines that the restoration is not yet over, which means the database will be available in Read Only mode and we can still apply subsequent backup files.

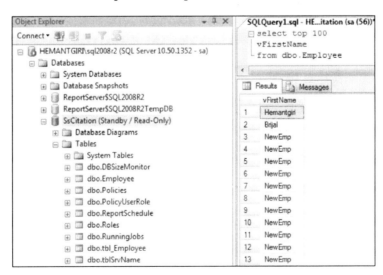

- ° **Delay Restoring backups at least**: This option will set the delay time before the next T-Log backup is applied to the secondary database.

- ○ **Alert if no restore occurs within:** This option specifies the time to wait until SQL Server triggers the alert, if no T-Log restoration occurs within the stipulated time.
- ○ **Restore job:** Here, we mention the name of the job to be restored and the schedule for T-Log restoration occurrence.

Setting Monitor Server instance

Now that we are done with setting the secondary database, let's configure Monitor Server by checking the **Use a monitor server instance** option as shown in the following screenshot:

Clicking on the **Settings...** button in the screenshot will bring up the window as shown here:

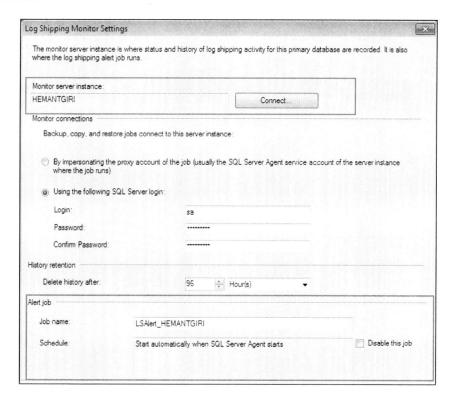

Clicking on the **Connect...** button will open a login dialog box to connect to the Monitor server instance. We need to specify the server we would like to act as the Monitor Server; enter the credentials, and click **Connect...**.

The next section of the **Log Shipping Monitor Settings** page is **Monitor connections** where we have to specify whether we are going to choose agent service account or SQL server login for backup, copy, and restore jobs that we have created in the previous section.

In the Alert job section, specify the job name if we want it to change and specify the history retention period for alert job.

Once we are done and have clicked **OK**, it will start the process of backing up the database on Primary Server, restoring backup to the Secondary Server, saving configuration for primary and secondary database, and also monitoring the server. We need to ensure that the report shows the success status for all of these processes as shown in the following screenshot:

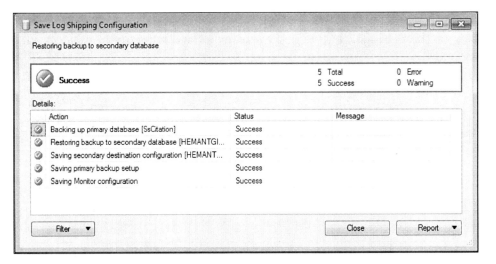

Configuration

Here is the T-SQL code to set up a primary and Secondary Server for Log Shipping. The scripts are generated by choosing the appropriate **Script Configuration...** option in the GUI window that appears after right-clicking on the database, and then selecting **Tasks | Ship Transaction Log**.

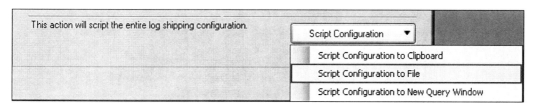

Setting up Primary Server for Log Shipping

So far we have learned how to install Log Shipping using GUI. Let's now see how to set up Primary Server for Log Shipping using the T-SQL script generated from SSMS.

```
Note: This chunk of code needs to be executed in a single execution/
single step

DECLARE @LS_BackupJobId AS uniqueidentifier
DECLARE @LS_PrimaryId   AS uniqueidentifier
DECLARE @SP_Add_RetCode As int

EXEC @SP_Add_RetCode = master.dbo.sp_add_log_shipping_primary_database

        @database = N'SsCitation'
        ,@backup_directory = N'\\hemantgiri\share'
        ,@backup_share = N'\\hemantgiri\share'
        ,@backup_job_name = N'LSBackup_SsCitation'
        -- Backup retention time mentioned in minutes
        ,@backup_retention_period = 4320
        -- If the Backup Compression is 2 it will use the setting of
the backup compression default value
        ,@backup_compression = 2
        ,@monitor_server = N'HEMANTGIRI'
        ,@monitor_server_security_mode = 0
        ,@monitor_server_login = N'**********'
        ,@monitor_server_password = N'**********'
        /*Backup threshold means, Agent will wait before it sends
out alert if backup does not occur
            within the time or threshold value specified
        */
        ,@backup_threshold = 60
        -- If Threshold alert enabled is 0, alert is disable and if
it is 1 alert is enable
        ,@threshold_alert_enabled = 1
        -- History retention period in minutes
```

```
              ,@history_retention_period = 5760
              -- This will be the backup job id for backup job on primary
server
              ,@backup_job_id = @LS_BackupJobId OUTPUT
              -- This will be the id of the primary database
              ,@primary_id = @LS_PrimaryId OUTPUT
              ,@overwrite = 1
```

The preceding chunk of code will create the backup job for the Log Shipping on the Primary Server. There are a few variables for which we need to change certain values according to the environment:

- `@database`: This is the name of the database for which we are configuring Log Shipping
- `@backup_directory`: The directory where we will place the Transaction log backup
- `@backup_Share`: This will be the location on the network where we can find the Transaction log backup
- `@backup_job_name`: This will be the name of the backup job
- `@monitor_server`: This will be the Monitor Server name
- `@monitor_server_login`: Login ID used to connect to the Monitor Server
- `@monitor_server_password`: Password used to connect to the Monitor Server
- `@schedule_name`: Name of the schedule for the backup job
- `@primary_database`: Name of the primary database
- `@secondary_server`: Name of the Secondary Server
- `@secondary_database`: Name of the secondary database

The following code will add a schedule to the job, previously created using `sp_add_log_shipping_primary_database`:

```
IF (@@ERROR = 0 AND @SP_Add_RetCode = 0)
BEGIN

DECLARE @LS_BackUpScheduleUID As uniqueidentifier
DECLARE @LS_BackUpScheduleID  AS int

EXEC msdb.dbo.sp_add_schedule
        @schedule_name =N'LSBackupSchedule_HEMANTGIRI1'
        ,@enabled = 1
        -- Frequency Type 4 means this job is configured to execute
daily
```

```
,@freq_type = 4
,@freq_interval = 1
/*
Frequency Subday type specifies the duration of the job to
get executed
here it is in minutes
*/
,@freq_subday_type = 4
/*
@freq_subday_interval value specify the period between two
execution
time of the job, here it is 15 and @freq_subday_type =4
means this job will be executed every 15 minutes
*/
,@freq_subday_interval = 15
/*
Need to specify the value only if the freq_type is either
weekly, monthly or monthly relative
*/
,@freq_recurrence_factor = 0
,@active_start_date = 20100610
,@active_end_date = 99991231
,@active_start_time = 0
,@active_end_time = 235900
,@schedule_uid = @LS_BackUpScheduleUID OUTPUT
,@schedule_id = @LS_BackUpScheduleID OUTPUT
```

The following procedure will attach the schedule that we have just created to the backup job created in the first part of the code:

```
EXEC msdb.dbo.sp_attach_schedule
        @job_id = @LS_BackupJobId
        ,@schedule_id = @LS_BackUpScheduleID

EXEC msdb.dbo.sp_update_job
        @job_id = @LS_BackupJobId
        ,@enabled = 1
```

This job will add an entry for the Secondary Server, into the Primary Server:

```
EXEC master.dbo.sp_add_log_shipping_primary_secondary
        @primary_database = N'SsCitation'
        ,@secondary_server = N'HEMANTGIRI\sql2008r2'
        ,@secondary_database = N'SSCitation'
        ,@overwrite = 1
```

Setting up Secondary Server

Execute this script on the Secondary Server:

```
DECLARE @LS_Secondary__CopyJobId    AS uniqueidentifier
DECLARE @LS_Secondary__RestoreJobId AS uniqueidentifier
DECLARE @LS_Secondary__SecondaryId  AS uniqueidentifier
DECLARE @LS_Add_RetCode As int

EXEC @LS_Add_RetCode = master.dbo.sp_add_log_shipping_secondary_
primary
        @primary_server = N'HEMANTGIRI'
        ,@primary_database = N'SsCitation'
        ,@backup_source_directory = N'\\hemantgiri\share'
        ,@backup_destination_directory = N'\\Hemantgiri\
LSDestination'
        ,@copy_job_name = N'LSCopy_HEMANTGIRI_SsCitation'
        ,@restore_job_name = N'LSRestore_HEMANTGIRI_SsCitation'
        -- File retention period in minutes
        ,@file_retention_period = 4320
        ,@monitor_server = N'HEMANTGIRI'

        ,@monitor_server_security_mode = 0
        ,@monitor_server_login = N'sa'
        ,@monitor_server_password = N'*********'
        ,@overwrite = 1
        ,@copy_job_id = @LS_Secondary__CopyJobId OUTPUT
        ,@restore_job_id = @LS_Secondary__RestoreJobId OUTPUT
        ,@secondary_id = @LS_Secondary__SecondaryId OUTPUT
```

This job will create a backup, and will restore T-Log backup files on the Secondary Server. Again, there are values that need to be changed according to our environment.

- @primary_server: Name of the Primary Server.

- @primary_database: Name of the primary database.

- @backup_source_directory: Location *from* where the copy job will copy the transaction log backup file.

- @backup_destination_directory: Location *to* where the copy job will place the transaction log backup file.

- @copy_job_name: Name of the copy transaction log backup file job.

- @restore_job_name: Name of the restore transaction log backup file job.

- @monitor_server: This will be the monitor sever name.

- `@schedule_name`: Name of the schedule for the copy and restore job.

- `@secondary_database`: Name of the secondary database.

- `@primary_server`: Name of the Primary Server.

- `@primary_databse`: Name of the primary database security mode for the monitor server. The value can either be 0 or 1, where 0 represents *SQL server authentication* and 1 represents *windows authentication mode*.

The following T-SQL code will add schedule for copy job that executes every 15 minutes on a daily basis:

```
IF (@@ERROR = 0 AND @LS_Add_RetCode = 0)
BEGIN


DECLARE @LS_SecondaryCopyJobScheduleUID    As uniqueidentifier
DECLARE @LS_SecondaryCopyJobScheduleID     AS int
```

This procedure will attach a schedule that we created in the previous code for copying job:

```
EXEC msdb.dbo.sp_add_schedule
        @schedule_name =N'DefaultCopyJobSchedule'
        ,@enabled = 1
        ,@freq_type = 4
        ,@freq_interval = 1
        ,@freq_subday_type = 4
        ,@freq_subday_interval = 15
        ,@freq_recurrence_factor = 0
        ,@active_start_date = 20100610
        ,@active_end_date = 99991231
        ,@active_start_time = 0
        ,@active_end_time = 235900
        ,@schedule_uid = @LS_SecondaryCopyJobScheduleUID OUTPUT
        ,@schedule_id = @LS_SecondaryCopyJobScheduleID OUTPUT


EXEC msdb.dbo.sp_attach_schedule
        @job_id = @LS_Secondary__CopyJobId
        ,@schedule_id = @LS_SecondaryCopyJobScheduleID
```

The following code will add schedule for restoring of T-Log job, and will execute every 15 minutes on a daily basis:

```
DECLARE @LS_SecondaryRestoreJobScheduleUID As uniqueidentifier
DECLARE @LS_SecondaryRestoreJobScheduleID  AS int

EXEC msdb.dbo.sp_add_schedule
        @schedule_name =N'DefaultRestoreJobSchedule'
        ,@enabled = 1
        ,@freq_type = 4
        ,@freq_interval = 1
        ,@freq_subday_type = 4
        ,@freq_subday_interval = 15
        ,@freq_recurrence_factor = 0
        ,@active_start_date = 20100610
        ,@active_end_date = 99991231
        ,@active_start_time = 0
        ,@active_end_time = 235900
        ,@schedule_uid = @LS_SecondaryRestoreJobScheduleUID OUTPUT
        ,@schedule_id = @LS_SecondaryRestoreJobScheduleID OUTPUT
```

This procedure will attach a schedule that we created in the previous code in order to restore the job:

```
EXEC msdb.dbo.sp_attach_schedule
        @job_id = @LS_Secondary__RestoreJobId
        ,@schedule_id = @LS_SecondaryRestoreJobScheduleID


END


DECLARE @LS_Add_RetCode2       As int


IF (@@ERROR = 0 AND @LS_Add_RetCode = 0)
BEGIN
/* This will setup a secondary database */
EXEC @LS_Add_RetCode2 = master.dbo.sp_add_log_shipping_secondary_
database
        @secondary_database = N'SSCitation'
        ,@primary_server = N'HEMANTGIRI'
        ,@primary_database = N'SsCitation'
        -- value of time server will wait before restoring next
backup file
```

```
          ,@restore_delay = 0
          -- if the value is 0 LS is setup using NoRecovery mode and
if its 1 the restore mode is Standby
          ,@restore_mode = 1
          /* If the disconnect users value is set to 1, all the users
that are connected will get disconnected at the time of
          restoration process */
          ,@disconnect_users  = 1
          -- threshold value before alert is raised if backup file
doesn't get restored
          ,@restore_threshold = 45
          ,@threshold_alert_enabled = 1
          -- History retention period in minute
          ,@history_retention_period = 5760
          ,@overwrite = 1

END



IF (@@error = 0 AND @LS_Add_RetCode = 0)
BEGIN

EXEC msdb.dbo.sp_update_job
          @job_id = @LS_Secondary__CopyJobId
          ,@enabled = 1

EXEC msdb.dbo.sp_update_job
          @job_id = @LS_Secondary__RestoreJobId
          ,@enabled = 1

END
```

 We can change the server name, database name, and other options according to our environment.

Summary

In this chapter we have learned what Log Shipping is, what different components it has, and the prerequisites for establishing Log Shipping. We also learned how it works and what the significance of establishing Log Shipping is. This will help us install and configure Log Shipping in an appropriate manner and troubleshoot the most common errors.

In the next chapter, we will learn how to install, configure, and troubleshoot common errors while using database mirroring.

8
Database Mirroring

Mr. Young, who is the Principal DBA in XY Incorporation, a large manufacturing company, was asked to come up with a solution that could serve his company's needs to make a database server highly available, without a manual or minimal human intervention. He was also asked to keep in mind the limited budget the company has for the financial year.

After careful research, he has come up with an idea to go with Database Mirroring as it provides an option of Automatic Failover—a cost effective solution. He has prepared a technical document for the management and peers, in order to make them understand how it works, based on tests he performed on virtual test servers. Here is the list of topics covered in this documentation:

- What is Database Mirroring
- Different components of Database Mirroring
- How Database Mirroring works
- What are the prerequisites of Database Mirroring
- How to install Database Mirroring
- How to configure Database Mirroring using T-SQL?

What is Database Mirroring

Database Mirroring is an option that can be used to cater to the business need, in order to increase the availability of SQL Server database as standby, for it to be used as an alternate production server in the case of any emergency. As its name suggests, **mirroring** stands for making an exact copy of the data. Mirroring can be done onto a disk, website, or somewhere else.

Similarly, Microsoft has introduced Database Mirroring with the launch of SQL Server 2005 post SP1, which performs the same function—making an exact copy of the database between two physically separate database servers. As Mirroring is a database-wide feature, it can be implemented per database instead of implementing it server wide.

 Disk Mirroring is a technology wherein data is stored on physically separate but identical hard disks at the same time called hardware array disk 1 or RAID 1.

Different components of the Database Mirroring

To install Database Mirroring, there are three components that are required. They are as follows:

- **Principal Server**: This is the database server that will send out the data to the participant server (we'll call it secondary/standby server) in the form of transactions.

- **Secondary Server**: This is the database server that receives all the transactions that are sent by the Principal Server in order to keep the database identical.

- **Witness Server (optional)**: This server will continuously monitor the Principal and Secondary Server and will enable automatic failover. This is an optional server.

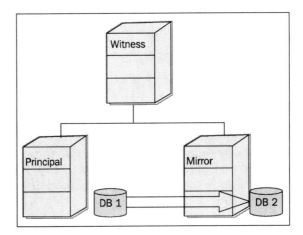

To have the automatic failover feature, the Principal Server should be in the synchronous mode.

How Database Mirroring works

In Database Mirroring, every server is a known partner and they complement each other as Principal and Mirror. There will be only one Principal and only one Mirror at any given time.

In reality, DML operations that are performed on the Principal Server are all re-performed at the Mirror server. As we all know, the data is written into the **Log Buffer** before it is written into data pages. Database Mirroring sends data that is written into Principal Server's Log Buffer simultaneously to the Mirror database. All these transactions are sent in a sequential manner and as quickly as possible.

There are two different operating modes at which Database Mirroring operates—asynchronous and synchronous.

Asynchronous a.k.a. High Performance mode

The transactions are sent to the Secondary Server as soon as they are written into the Log Buffer. In this mode of operation, the data is first committed at the Principal Server before it actually is written into the Log Buffer of the Secondary Server. Hence this mode is called **High Performance** mode, but at the same time, it introduces a chance of data loss.

Synchronous a.k.a. High Safety mode

The transactions are sent to the Secondary Server as soon as they are written to the Log Buffer. These transactions are then committed simultaneously at both the ends.

Prerequisites

Let's now have a look at the prerequisite to have Database Mirroring in place. Please be cautious with the prerequisites, as a single missed requisite would result in a failure in installation.

- **Recovery Mode**: To implement Database Mirroring, the database should be in the Full Recovery mode.

- **Initialization of database**: The database on which to install Database Mirroring should be present in the mirror database. To achieve this, we can restore the most recent backup, followed by the transaction log with the **NORECOVERY** option.

- **Database name**: Ensure that the database name is the same for both, the principal as well as the mirror database.

- **Compatibility**: Ensure that the partner servers are on the same edition of the SQL Server. Database Mirroring is supported by the Standard and Enterprise edition.

> Synchronous mode with Automatic failover is an Enterprise-only feature.

- **Disk space**: Ensure that we have ample space available for the mirror database.

- **Service accounts**: Ensure that the service accounts that we have used are domain accounts and they have the required permission, that is, CONNECT permission to the endpoints.

- **Listener port**: These are TCP ports on which a Database Mirroring session is established between the Principal and Mirror server.

- **Endpoints:** These are the objects that are dedicated to Database Mirroring and enable the SQL Server to communicate over the network.

- **Authentication**: While both the Principal and Mirror servers talk to each other, they should authenticate each other. For this, the accounts that we use — local accounts or domain accounts — should have login and send message permissions. If the accounts we use are using local logins as service accounts, we must use **Certificates** to authenticate a connection request.

Installing Database Mirroring

In the previous section, we learned about the prerequisites to install Database Mirroring; let's now learn how to install it.

Preparing for Database Mirroring

Before we move forward, we shall prepare the database for the Database Mirroring. Here are the steps:

1. The first step is to ensure that the database is in Full Recovery mode. You can set the mode to "Full Recovery" using the following code:

```
SQLQuery1.sql
   USE MASTER
   GO
   ALTER DATABASE AdventureWorks
   SET RECOVERY FULL
   GO
```

2. Execute the backup command, followed by the transaction log backup command, and move the backups to the server we wish to have as a mirror.

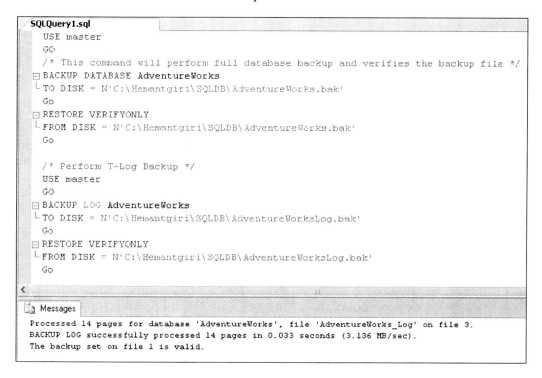

```
SQLQuery1.sql
   USE master
   GO
   /* This command will perform full database backup and verifies the backup file */
   BACKUP DATABASE AdventureWorks
   TO DISK = N'C:\Hemantgiri\SQLDB\AdventureWorks.bak'
   Go
   RESTORE VERIFYONLY
   FROM DISK = N'C:\Hemantgiri\SQLDB\AdventureWorks.bak'
   Go


   /* Perform T-Log Backup */
   USE master
   GO
   BACKUP LOG AdventureWorks
   TO DISK = N'C:\Hemantgiri\SQLDB\AdventureWorksLog.bak'
   Go
   RESTORE VERIFYONLY
   FROM DISK = N'C:\Hemantgiri\SQLDB\AdventureWorksLog.bak'
   Go
```

```
Messages
Processed 14 pages for database 'AdventureWorks', file 'AdventureWorks_Log' on file 3.
BACKUP LOG successfully processed 14 pages in 0.033 seconds (3.136 MB/sec).
The backup set on file 1 is valid.
```

 I have run the RESTORE VERIFYONLY command after backup completes. This command ensures the validity of a backup file. It is recommended to always verify the backup.

3. As we have a full database and log backup file, move them over to the Mirror server that we have identified.

4. We will now perform the database restoration, followed by the restore log command with **NORECOVERY**.

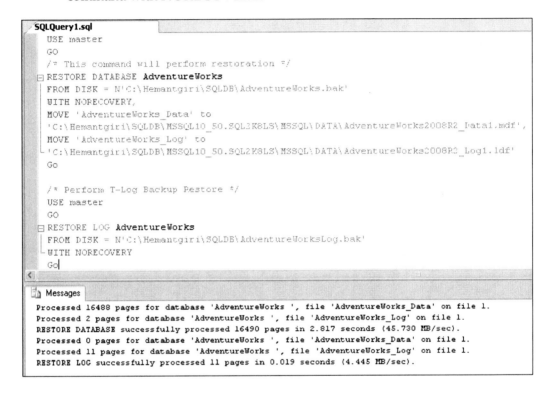

```
SQLQuery1.sql
  USE master
  GO
  /* This command will perform restoration */
  RESTORE DATABASE AdventureWorks
  FROM DISK = N'C:\Hemantgiri\SQLDB\AdventureWorks.bak'
  WITH NORECOVERY,
  MOVE 'AdventureWorks_Data' to
  'C:\Hemantgiri\SQLDB\MSSQL10_50.SQL2K8LS\MSSQL\DATA\AdventureWorks2008R2_Data1.mdf',
  MOVE 'AdventureWorks_Log' to
  'C:\Hemantgiri\SQLDB\MSSQL10_50.SQL2K8LS\MSSQL\DATA\AdventureWorks2008R2_Log1.ldf'
  Go

  /* Perform T-Log Backup Restore */
  USE master
  GO
  RESTORE LOG AdventureWorks
  FROM DISK = N'C:\Hemantgiri\SQLDB\AdventureWorksLog.bak'
  WITH NORECOVERY
  Go
```

```
Messages
Processed 16488 pages for database 'AdventureWorks ', file 'AdventureWorks_Data' on file 1.
Processed 2 pages for database 'AdventureWorks ', file 'AdventureWorks_Log' on file 1.
RESTORE DATABASE successfully processed 16490 pages in 2.817 seconds (45.730 MB/sec).
Processed 0 pages for database 'AdventureWorks ', file 'AdventureWorks_Data' on file 1.
Processed 11 pages for database 'AdventureWorks ', file 'AdventureWorks_Log' on file 1.
RESTORE LOG successfully processed 11 pages in 0.019 seconds (4.445 MB/sec).
```

 It is necessary to use the NORECOVERY option so that additional log backups or transactions can be applied.

Installing Database Mirroring

As the database that we want to participate in the Database Mirroring is now ready, we can move on with the actual installation process.

1. Right-click on the database we want to mirror and select **Tasks | Mirror...**.

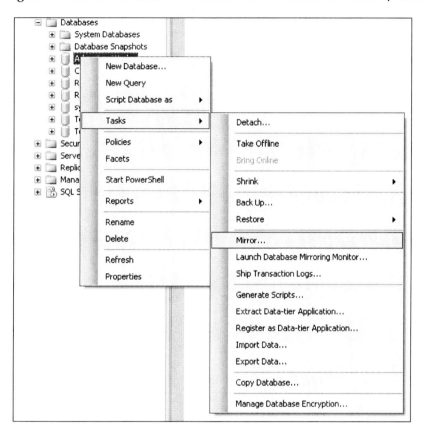

2. It will open the following screen. To start with the actual setup, click on the **Configure Security...** button.

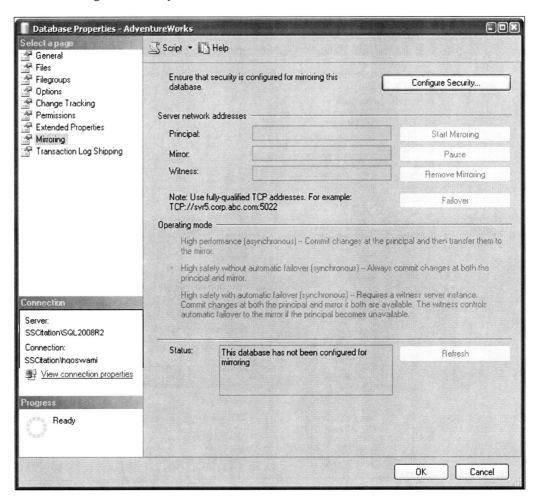

3. In this dialog box, select the **No** option as we are not including the Witness Server at this stage and will be performing this task later.

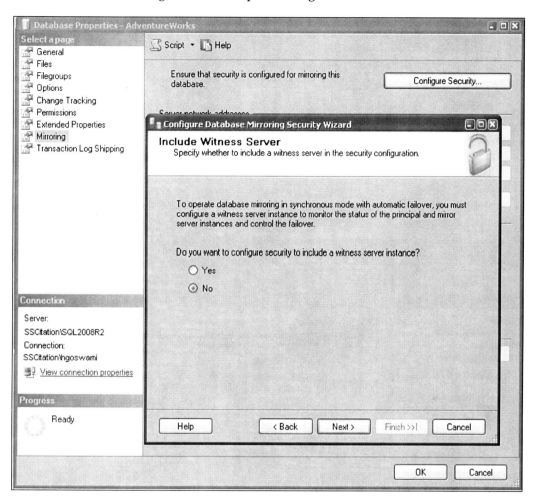

4. In the next dialog box, connect to the **Principal Server**. Specify the **Listener Port** and **Endpoint name**, and click **Next**.

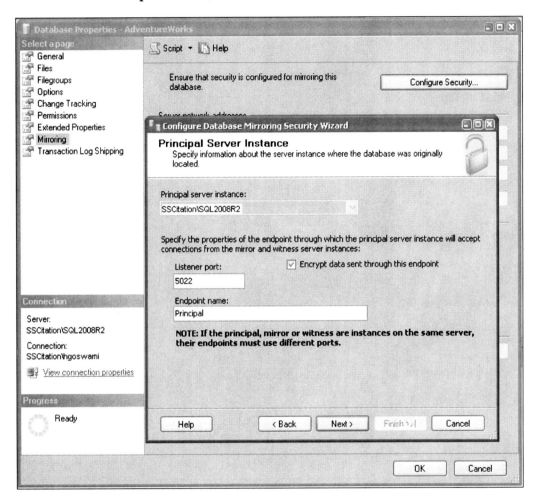

5. We are now asked to configure the property for the **Mirror Server, Listener port**, and **Endpoint name**.

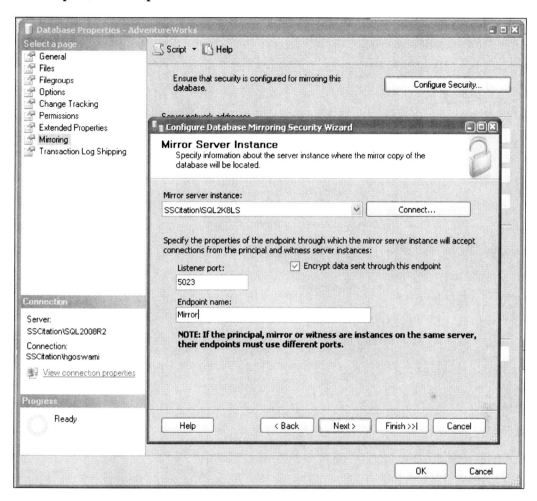

6. In this step, the installation wizard asks us to specify the service account that will be used by the Database Mirroring operation.

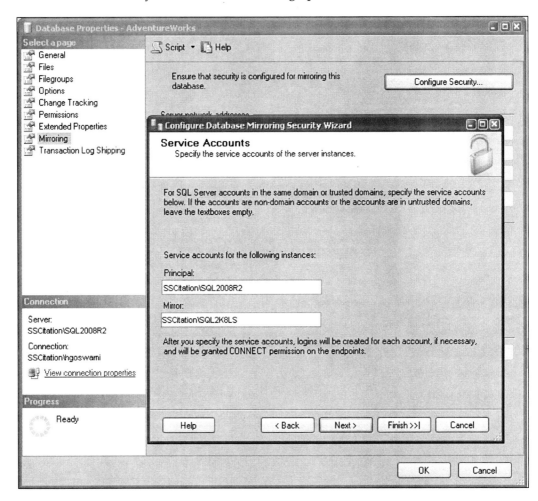

If a person is using local system account as a service account, he/she must use **Certificates** for authentication. Generally, these certificates are used by the websites to assure their users that the information is secured. Certificates are the digital documents that store digital signature or identity information of the holder for authenticity purpose. They ensure that every byte of information being sent over the internet/intranet/vpn, and stored at the server, is safe. Certificates are installed at the servers, either by obtaining them from the providers such as www.thwate.com or can be self-issued by Database Administrator or Chief Information Officer of the company using the httpcfg.exe utility. The same is true for SQL Server. SQL Server uses certificates to ensure that the information is secured and these certificates can be issued by self, using httpcfg. exe, or can be obtained from issuing authority. Refer to *Appendix B, External References*, for an article on this.

7. In the next dialog box, make sure that the configuration details we have furnished are valid. Ensure that the name of the Principal and Mirror Server, Endpoints, and port number are correct. Click **Finish**.

8. Ensure that the setup wizard returns a success report at the end.

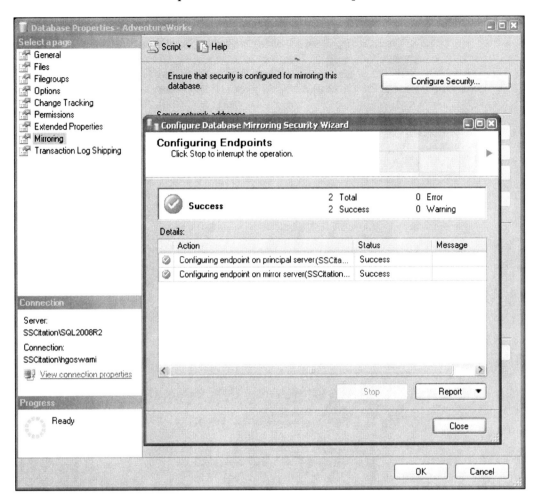

Starting Database Mirroring

Once we are done preparing for and installing Database Mirroring, we can start with the actual Database Mirroring. Please follow the steps, as mentioned here:

1. As soon as the setup wizard finishes, we will be presented with the option to start mirroring. Please note that the **Operating mode** is set as **High safety without automatic failover (synchronous)**.

The transactions are written in the synchronous mode of operating, and they commit on Principal and Mirror at the same time.

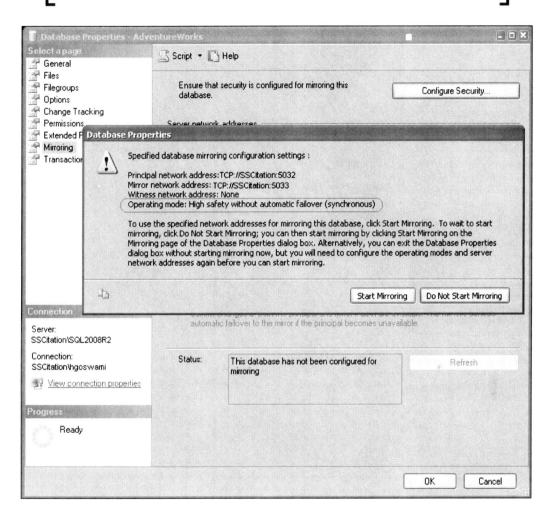

2. In the next step, we can change the operating mode of the Database Mirroring we have configured and/or we can pause or remove the mirroring, if we wish to do so for any reason.

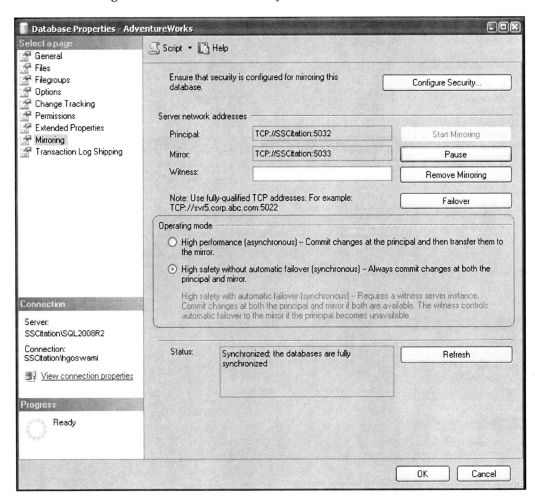

3. As we are done with the Mirroring installation, let's check the status of the databases on the Principal and Mirror server.

   In the following snapshot, the left-hand side shows the Principal Server; notice that the database status shows **Principal, Synchronized**. The right-hand side shows the Mirror server. Notice again that the database status is **Restoring....**, which means there are transactions that could be applied on the mirrored database, running in the single user mode.

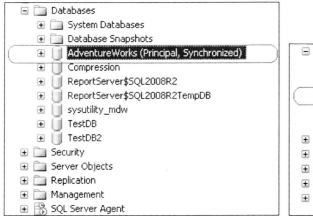 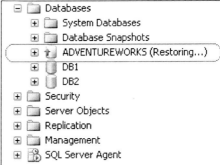

Manual or forced failover

Until now, we have learned how to install Database Mirroring. Now let's see how to failover manually just to ensure that the installation went fine and is working properly.

1. Right-click the database name we have configured for mirroring, and from the options, select **Tasks | Mirror**. This will bring the main configuration dialog box for Database Mirroring. Once there, click on the **Failover** button. It will then ask us to confirm whether or not we wish to proceed with failover; click **Yes**.

At this stage, [local\SQL2008R2] is **Principal** server and [local\SQL2008LS] is the **Mirror** server.

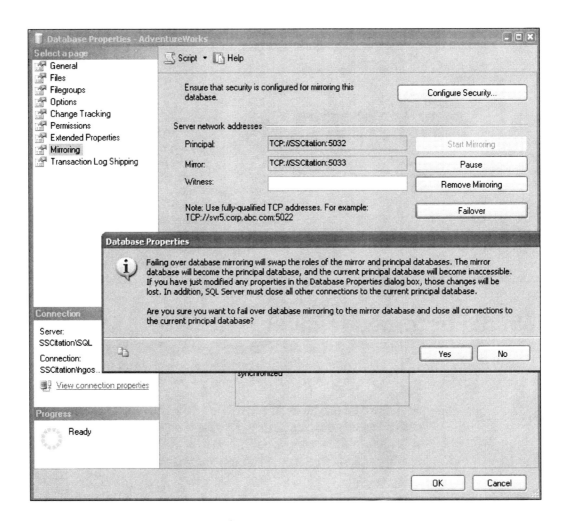

2. In the next screenshot, notice that the status of the database on the instance [local\SQL2008R2] has been changed to **Mirror, Synchronized / Restoring...**, whereas database status on the instance [local\SQL2K8LS] has been changed to **Principal, Synchronized**.

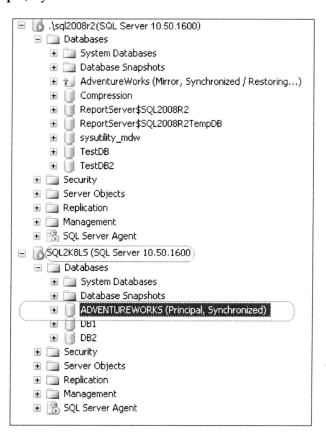

Adding the Witness Server

We have not included the Witness Server while we installed Database Mirroring, as we want it to be added later, once we finish with the installation. The reason was, what if we don't have a server that we can configure as a Witness Server while installing Database Mirroring? Can we add a Witness Server later? Well, the answer is Yes, and here is how we go about adding a Witness Server:

1. Right-click on the database we have configured for Database Mirroring and select **Tasks | Mirror**. From the setup dialog box, click on configuration. It will ask us if we want to include the Witness Server; this time, select the **Yes** option and then click **Next**.

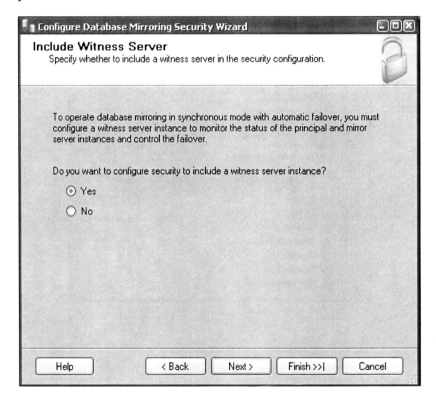

2. In the next dialog box, choose the server to configure. Here, select **Witness Server instance** and click **Next**.

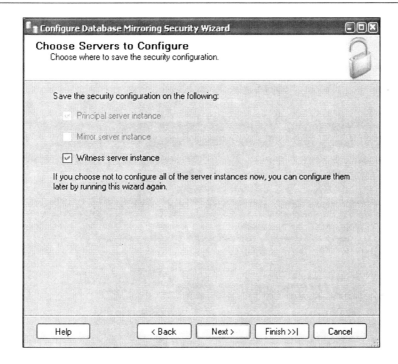

3. As we have failed over, the **Principal server instance** is now
   [local\SQL2K8LS]. Click **Next**.

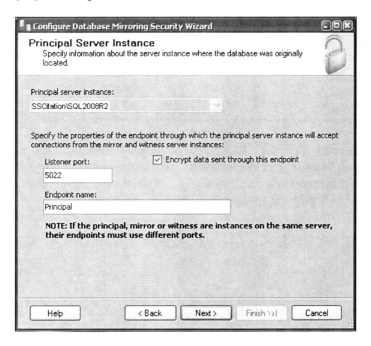

On the Mirror server, we have named the endpoint as **Mirror** when we installed Database Mirroring. So, do not get confused by these names as these names have been chosen for better understanding.

4. In the **Witness Server Instance** dialog box, specify the name of the Witness Server instance. As can be seen from the following screenshot, I have named the instance on my server as **[local\Witness]**, which has the **Endpoint name** as **WITNESS** and it listens on port **5034**.

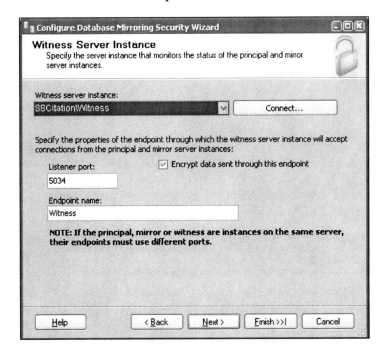

5. In the **Service Accounts** dialog box, enter the service account names for the **Principal**, **Mirror**, and **Witness** servers. Ensure that this service account is a domain account and has the necessary permission, that is, the CONNECT permission for the endpoint database role. Click **Next**.

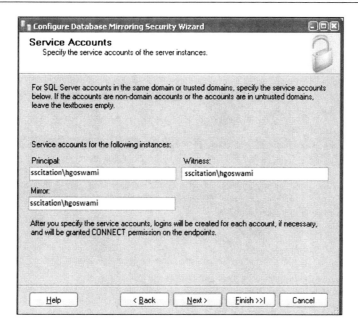

6. In the next dialog box, ensure that the information furnished while including the Witness Server is correct and click **Finish** to complete the wizard.

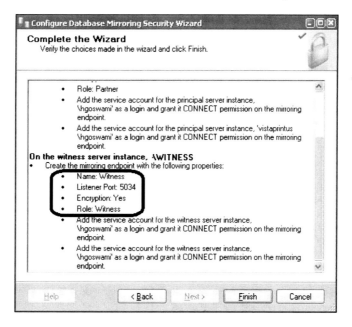

Configuration using T-SQL

We have seen how to install Database Mirroring using the wizard. It's now time to see Database Mirroring installation using T-SQL code.

1. The first step is to create an endpoint and a listener port on the Principal Server.

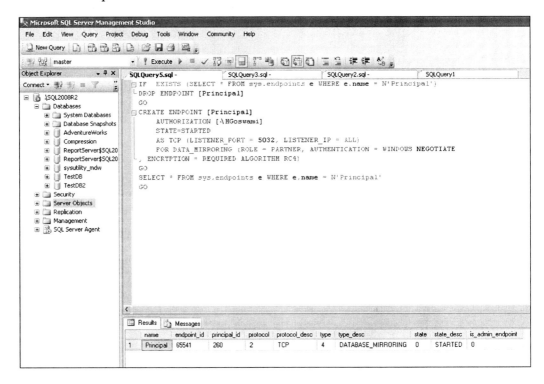

2. The next step is to create the endpoint and listener port on the Mirror instance. To do so, execute the following code on the Mirror server:

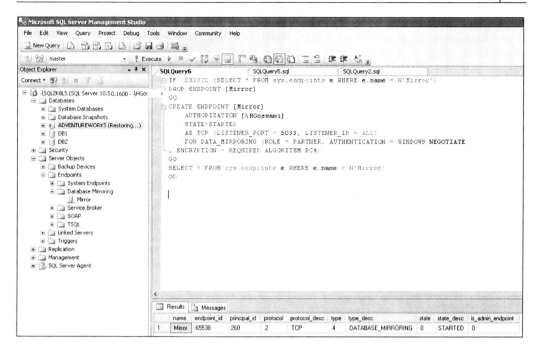

3. We will now create a partner for the database that we want to be part of the Database Mirroring setup. Execute the code shown in the next screenshot into the Mirror server to establish the Mirroring session:

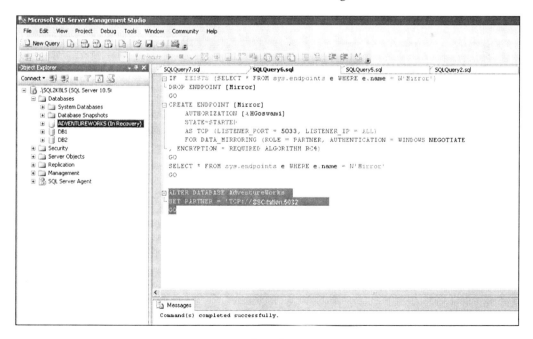

4. In the next step, we will create a partnership for the Mirror server, by executing the code shown in the following screenshot:

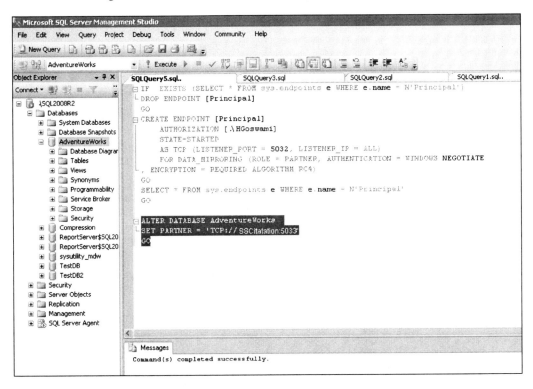

5. To failover using the T-SQL command, execute the following command, and it will initiate failover:

Automatic failover is an enterprise-specific feature and will be available when we have included the Witness Server. The Witness Server does the work of monitoring the availability of the Principal Server, and as soon as it doesn't receive an acknowledgement, it initiates the failover process.

Monitoring the Database Mirroring status using Database Mirroring Monitor

While using Database Mirroring, we can use Database Mirroring Monitor periodically to see how it is performing. Here is how we do it:

Right-click on the database we have mirrored and select **Tasks | Launch Database Mirror Monitor**.

This brings the mirroring monitor, which gives information on unsent or unrestored logs (if any) along with the oldest unsent transaction information.

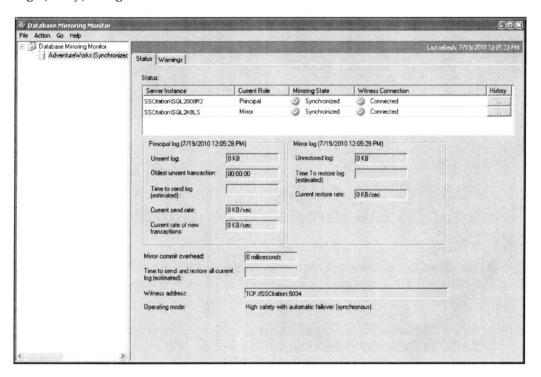

I have executed the UPDATE command and they have been recorded here; check the highlighted area.

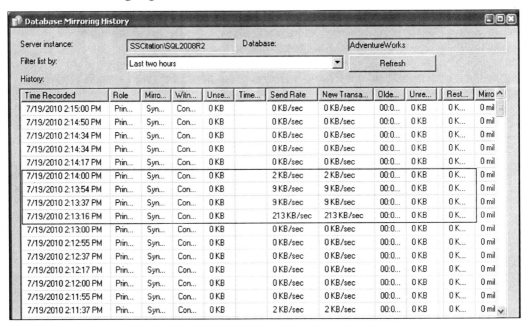

Configuring the threshold for Database Mirroring

It is always easy to troubleshoot if we get alerts for various errors or warnings, and Database Mirror is no exception. Let's see how to configure the threshold for the Database Mirroring.

1. On the **Database Mirroring Monitor** screen, select the **Warnings** tab and then click on the **Set Thresholds...** button at the bottom-right side.

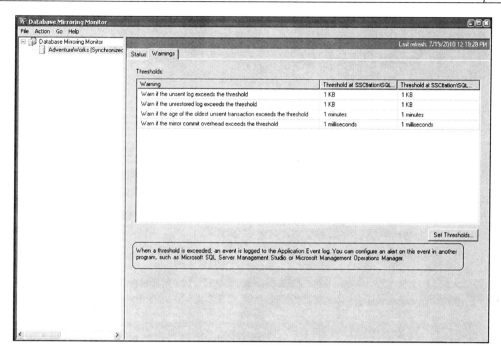

2. On the **Set Warning Thresholds** screen, check and enable the warning we want to observe and click on the **Threshold at** listbox to alter the value. Once we are done with the altering of the value, click **OK** to exit.

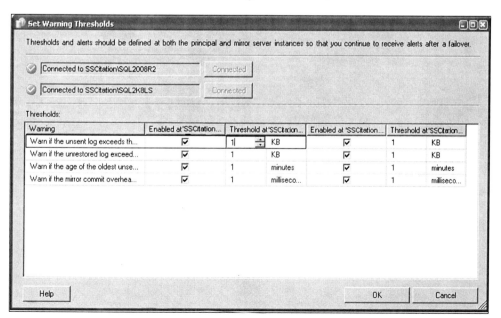

3. If we want to receive an alert using an alternate way, we can use the native Alert feature of SSMS. To configure Alert for database mirroring:

    i.   Expand the SQL Server Agent.

    ii. Expand the Alerts node.

    iii. Right-click on **Alerts** and select **New Alert**.

    iv. Enter the name of the alert.

    v.   Mention the type of alert as **SQL Server Performance condition alert**.

    vi. Select the object in the form Instance Name: Database Mirroring. In our case, it will be **MSSQL$SQL2008R2: Database Mirroring**.

    vii. Select **Transaction Delay** as the value for **Counter**; we may define any other object as per requirement.

    viii.Select the database name as the value for **Instance**.

4. Set the counter value. The default value is **10** (as shown in the screenshot), and we can change this value based on the environment and requirement.

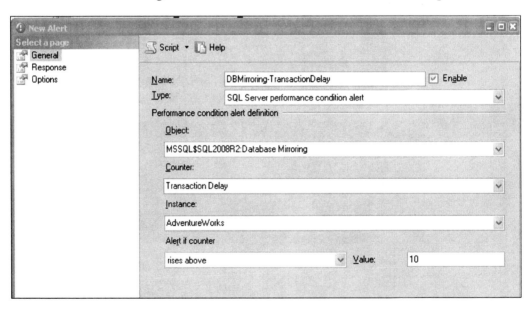

5. Click on the **Response** option in the left-hand corner, which will bring the screen shown in the following screenshot. Here, we have to select the operator to send a notification to, along with a means of notification; we have selected to notify the operator via e-mail. Click **OK**.

Alternatively, we may execute same job by checking the **Execute job** option.

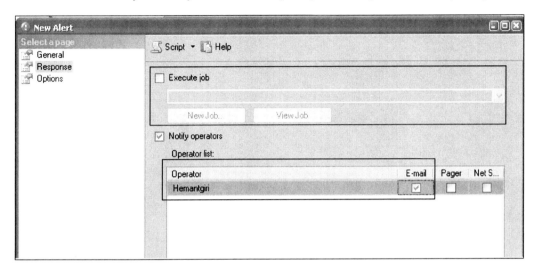

Summary

In this chapter, we learned what database mirroring is, how it works, and what are the prerequisites to install Database Mirroring. We also looked at how to install Database Mirroring and how to configure it using T-SQL.

Troubleshooting

This appendix lists all chapter-specific troubleshooting manuals.

Chapter 2: Implementing Clustering

Common troubleshooting—installation

Any time during setup if we encounter an error, we have to locate the installation summary file to troubleshoot the installation error. This summary file is located at `%programfiles%\Microsoft SQL Server\100\bootstrap\log`.

Network binding order

This error/warning is observed most often while installing failover cluster. To overcome this problem, we should correct the network order before installing failover cluster. The following are steps to perform that:

1. Go to **Start | Control Panel | Network and Internet | Network and Sharing Center**.

2. Click **Change Adapter Setting** on the left menu.

3. Press *Alt + F* and the **Advanced** menu will be visible to us.

4. Click **Advanced** settings; this will bring the dialog box wherein we can change the order of the network card.

5. Move the network card up on which we have configured the public network.

Problem while adding a second node

While installing a second node, we may face the error that may block our path to add a second node to the cluster.

We may face the error message **Failover instance MSSQLServer cluster group not found**, when the SQL Server Agent is not the part of cluster. To overcome this error and to proceed further successfully, we should manually change the registry by following Wael A. Kabli's blog entry: `http://blogs.msdn.com/wael/ archive/2009/12/07/cannot-add-a-second-node-to-an-sql-server-2008-failover-cluster.aspx`.

- **Current SKU is invalid**:

  While adding a second node, this error might show up; however, this was fixed with the first release of Cumulative Fix 50003415. Although there is another work around for this, if we are installing from the media that comes with Product Key embedded in it, then perform the following steps:

  1. Dump the CD/DVD setup on the local disk.
  2. Locate `defaultsetup.ini`.
  3. Cut and paste this file to some other location.
  4. Rerun `setup.exe` from the local disk.

- **All cluster disks available to this virtual server are owned by other node(s)**:

  This error comes when the cluster disks are owned by the other node; to resolve this error we should move the disk to the local node.

Common troubleshooting and tips—resources

Although DBAs always keep an eye on the Windows Event Viewer and SQL Server Error Log to monitor what is going on with the SQL Box, I would like to list some of the most common errors seen with Clustering.

- **Error**: SQL Server cannot log on to the Network after it migrates to another node as it is not able to contact the domain controller.

  Resolution: We should check if there is a problem with the trust relationship with the cluster node and domain controller. The other reason could be the network congestion or DNS.

- **Error**: SQL Server can't access the cluster disks.

  Resolution: Check if the firmware and drivers for the disks are the same on both the nodes.

- **Error**: Failure of SQL Server Services or SQL Server Agent Services.

  Resolution: There could be several reasons for this, but the most common ones are:

  ○ Check if the password has been changed recently but not updated in services property.

  ○ The Services account is locked out or disabled.

  ○ Sometimes Network/Security Administrator re-applies the NTFS permission on the MS SQL Server folder after the audit, and some-times it wipes out the existing permission. We have to see if the services account has the proper permission on the MS SQL Server folder and subfolders.

  ○ Sometimes it returns errors that are related to protocols initialization error. Here are some links to resolve this issue (although these are for SQL Server 2005 it should work for SQL Server 2008):

    `http://support.microsoft.com/kb/956378`

    `http://blogs.msdn.com/sql_protocols/archive/2007/02/01/ tdssniclient-initialization-failed-with-error-0x50- status-code-0x50.aspx`

    `http://blogs.msdn.com/sql_protocols/ archive/2006/01/10/511330.aspx`

- **Error:** Changing the IP address of Failover SQL Server cluster returned error.

  Resolution: The resolution is simple. What we should do is bring the SQL IP address and SQL network name offline, and then change the IP address and again bring the SQL IP address and SQL network online.

- **Error**: The IP address is already in use.

  Resolution: This error explains itself; the IP address we are trying to assign is already in use and hence we should procure another IP address and then assign.

- **Error**: The SQL Server failover cluster instance name could not be found as cluster resources.

  Resolution: Check whether the registry value for `<instld>\Cluster\ClusterName` is correct.

Chapter 3: Snapshot Replication

- **Question**: I get the following error: **Cannot make the change because a snapshot is already generated. Set** `@force_invalidate_snapshot` **to** 1**, in order to force the change and invalidate the existing snapshot**. How do I resolve this error?

  Answer: When we add an article to an existing publication that we have already initialized, now as we have added one more article to it, snapshot will become obsolete and will have be reinitialized to incorporate the changes. Adding parameter `@force_invalidate_snapshot=1` will force snapshot to be regenerated.

- **Question**: Every time I add an article, entire snapshot is generated. Why is that so?

  Answer: There is a property called `@immediate_sync` in the publication that enforces full snapshot to be generated immediately whenever a new article is added. Setting the value to `false` for the `@immediate_sync` will generate snapshot for only the newly added article.

  Execute the following command at the Publisher end to reset the value for `@immediate_sync` option:

  ```
  sp_changepublication @publication='publicationname',
  @property='immediate_sync',@value='FALSE'
  ```

  In this case, do not forget to call `sp_addsubscription` procedure for every subscription so that a newly added article can be added. And finally, call `sp_refreshsubscriptions` to refresh the existing Subscribers.

- **Question**: Why did Snapshot Agent fail to start?

  Answer: This question is often found in many newsgroups and various SQL Server forums. Most often this error is caused by login failure error or if there is an issue with the NTFS or share permissions. We need to make sure that we have given appropriate permission for both share and NTFS.

- **Question:** My snapshot has returned the following error: initial snapshot timeout.

  Answer: This means that the snapshot that has been generated is large enough or we may have an issue with the network (network congestion or DNS, among others). To overcome this problem:
    - Split the single publication into smaller and multiple publications
    - Compress the snapshot files
    - Increase the value of query timeout

 For more information on Agent Profile parameters, refer to the *Snapshot Agent parameters* section in Chapter 3.

- **Question**: Why has my transaction log grown so big?

  Answer: Replication is using BCP In and BCP Out to synchronize database. Also, BCP operations are fully logged under Full Recovery model and minimally logged when database is set to bulk-logged mode. It all results in all the transactions getting logged, making the transaction log to grow bigger in size.

  Although we may change the database recovery model to bulk-logged mode during bulk operation, it is not recommended as it affects the point-in-time recovery. The recommendation is that we should schedule T-Log backup for regular intervals at minimum latency, for example, every 15 minutes, so that we can have point-in-time recovery and we can also keep our T-log in shape.

Troubleshooting using Replication Monitor (RM)

When it comes to troubleshooting replication apart from troubleshooting it by viewing error details in the job history, we can use RM to troubleshoot errors. RM can be handy to identify the error details and to troubleshoot them.

1. To launch RM, call `sqlmonitor.exe`. Expand **My Publisher | PublisherName | Publication Name,** and select the **Agent** tab in the right-hand side pane.

2. Right-click on the **Agent** and select **View Details**; here we will see the summary option in the grid on the right-hand side of pane. If we click the drop-down arrow of the **View** option, we will be asked to choose an option from various available options.

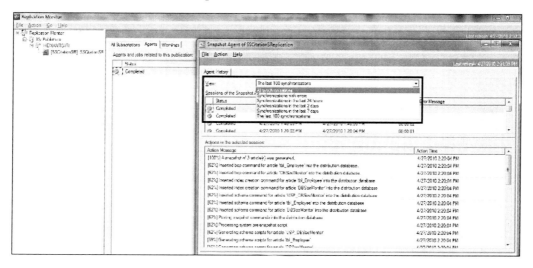

3. Until we have all successful synchronization, let's Un-share the folder where we have stored the snapshot files. Please refer to the following screenshot. The following screen represents the scenario after we have un-shared the snapshot share (also notice the red-cross on the Publisher).

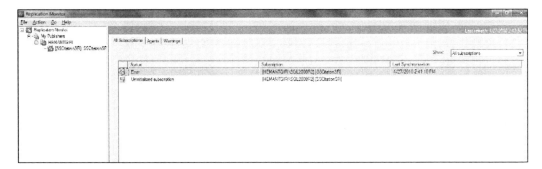

4. Right-click on the **Error** and select **View Details**. Notice the error message in the following screenshot; it clearly indicates that it could not find the network path.

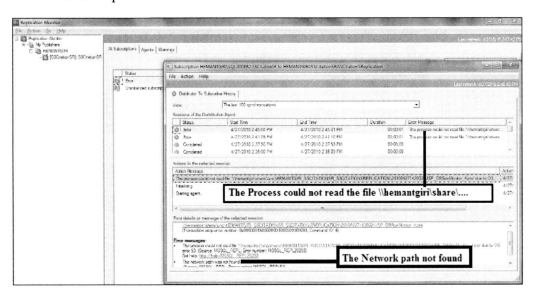

5. Let's re-share the folder and restore the share and NTFS permission. Notice that the snapshot has now been applied successfully.

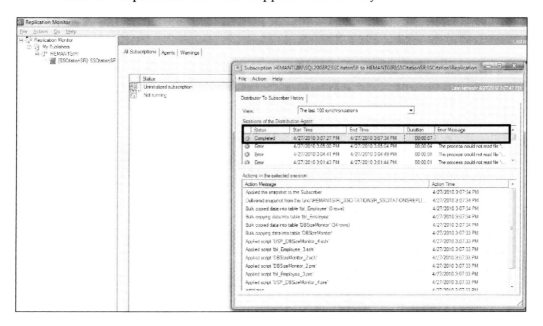

Chapter 4: Transactional Replication

*   **Question:** I have two subscriptions configured and one of them is not working, what should I check?

    Answer: We should check if the distribution agent is running, and check if there are any errors reported. If required try to reinitialize subscription and use replication monitor to watch what is happening.

*   **Question:** I get the following error: **Insert failed because of conflict with identity range check constraint**. How do I solve it?

    Answer: We should be careful when we use Identity with replication. Ideally we should manually assign the range at both the ends — Publisher and Subscriber — if we are using updatable subscription. Also, it is to be noted that Identity keys and triggers should be marked as **Not for Replication**.

> Here are the URLs of two good articles on managing Identity values in replication: `http://msdn.microsoft.com/en-us/library/ms152543.aspx` and `http://www.simple-talk.com/sql/database-administration/the-identity-crisis-in-replication/`.

- **Question:** OLEDB provider "SQLNCLI" for linked server "XXXX" returned message as **No transaction is alive** (.NET SqlClientData provider).

  Answer: We need to make sure that we have configured SQL Server Agent to run using domain account and not "local system" or "network services" account, as this account would have different SID on each machine and they would not be able to access common network resources.

- **Question:** Sometime I see an error "Subscription(s) have been marked as inactive and must be reinitialized, NoSync subscriptions will need to be dropped and recreated". How do I solve it?

  Answer: In most cases, re-intializing will work, and if not, query the system table Mssubscriptions and note down the record for which status = 0. If you find such an entry, execute a code mentioned here:

```
update distribution..MSsubscriptions set status = 2 where
publisher_id = 'VALUE'
and
publisher_db = 'SSCitationSR'
and
publication_id = 'VALUE'
and
subscriber_id = 'VALUE'
and
subscriber_db = 'DB_NAME'
```

 Note: This should be executed in case of the last option as this modifies the entry in the system table. As a first aid, we should try to a make fake update so that the initialization will get triggered or check if modifying the retention period can be of any help. If this option doesn't work, re-initialize the subscription.

- **Question:** I get the following error message: **Log Reader Agent failed to construct a replicated command from Log Sequence Number (LSN)**. How do I resolve it?

  Answer: Query the sysarticles table at the Publisher server and note down the name of the article if it shows value missing in the column filter. Note down the article name, remove it from the publication, and then re-add them. Once you re-add them, re-initialize the snapshot and it should work fine.

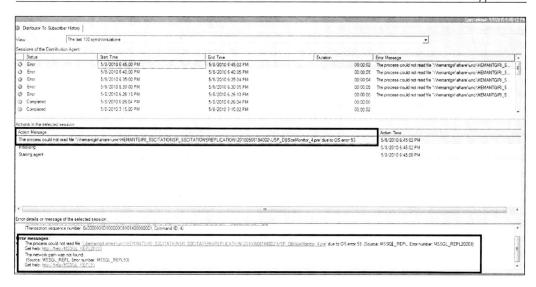

Chapter 5: Merge Replication

Index on columns used in filters

It is important to create index on the columns that are used for filtering and joins so as to perform faster retrieval of data. Whenever merge agent runs, it searches for the data, if database engine finds an index on the columns that are used for filter and join it can make the retrieval faster, otherwise it would have to search through the table.

Reference article on index:

I would strongly recommend reading the article on index(s) available at http://technet.microsoft.com/en-us/library/cc966523.aspx. This is the best ever article I have read on index(s); although for SQL Server 2000 it is equally true and applicable for any other version of SQL Server. The following are some more articles that could be of assistance:

- http://blogs.technet.com/josebda/archive/2009/03/17/indexing-best-practices-for-sql-server-2008.aspx

- http://research.microsoft.com/pubs/115263/ICDE10_conf_full_294.pdf

- http://sqlblogcasts.com/blogs/ssqanet/archive/2008/02/19/sql-server-2005-index-optimization-best-practices.aspx

- http://sqlserverpedia.com/blog/sql-server-bloggers/my-top-5-sql-server-indexing-best-practices/

LOB data types

Microsoft recommends that we should separate the columns that have LOB as data type to another table using a one-to-one relationship. This would help us reduce the overhead on performance.

Avoid using identity column as primary key

There has been a lot said about using identity as primary key in replicated database. The primary issue behind this is the manageability—every time identity value reaches its threshold value, we will have to reseed the identity value and adjust identity range at Publisher end; this happens when we restore backup at Subscriber end. We will have to find the last inserted identity value and adjust the identity range at Publisher using the following steps:

```
/* Step 1: Execute below T-SQL for every subscriber
*/
selectident_current('tblName')
go


/* Step 2 :Note down the highest value
found from subscribers
*/


/*
Step 3 : Execute below T-SQL at publisher
*/

dbcc checkident('tblName',reseed,value+1)
-- Note: value = heighest value found in step 1


/*
Step 4: At publisher execute below T-SQL
*/
executesp_adjustpublisherIdentityrange PublicationName, tblName
```

> Here is an article on my blog for reference, suggesting why not to use identity as PK: http://www.sql-server-citation.com/2009/12/common-mistakes-in-sql-server-part-2.html.

Frequently asked questions

- **Question**: I get the following message: **Violation of Primary Key**. And now I am unable to add a new value. So, how do I resolve it?

  Answer: As we are all aware, the primary key violation may occur only if there is a conflict of key value, and we should be careful while troubleshooting this error. Typically, we should check the following:

  - If the identity column is used, whether it is set to the "not for replication" option
  - Whether the identity management is auto or manual and what is the range specified
  - Is there any schema difference in any of the Subscriber and/or with Publisher
  - Check whether the duplicate record exists, and if yes, act accordingly

  There are so many reasons depending on the situation, but I would certainly recommend referring to an article by Hilary Cotter, available at `http://www.simple-talk.com/sql/database-administration/the-identity-crisis-in-replication/`.

- **Question**: Sometimes I notice the following error: **The Schema script 'some file name' could not propagated to the subscriber (Error number: -2142010001)** or **OS Error 2** or **System cannot find the file specified**. Why is it so?

  Answer: Ensure that the agent account responsible to run the merge account has the required (read, list and write) share and NTFS permission to the snapshot folder.

- **Question**: Why does Merge Agent or Distribution Agent keep on getting timeout error?

  Answer: To overcome the problem, go to **Agent Properties** and change the value of `QueryTimeOut` parameter as shown in the following screenshot:

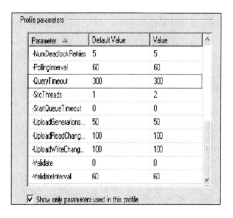

This is what we generally do, but there could be other factors that may have caused these errors such as number uploads size of row, the latency, or the network congestion. I recommend analyzing any error thoroughly before applying a solution.

Chapter 6: Peer-to-Peer Replication

- **Question**: While replicating LOB data, I get an error that reads **The Distribution Agent is using the OLEDB streaming optimization for replicating binary large objects (LOB) greater than %1!d! byres**. How can I resolve this?

  Answer: Increase the value for `-OledbStreamThreshold` using command line or creating a new agent profile.

- **Question**: We would like to implement the P2P replication but we don't have the domain environment. What type of account should we use?

  Answer: You may use the identical windows username and password on the systems participating in replication, or you may use SQL Server account for replication.

- **Question**: The following error appears in the error log "Index xxx is on table msXXX does not exist". How do I resolve this?

  Answer: You should check carefully if the index on the specified table exists. If not, you will have to drop and recreate the publication

- **Question**: Peer-to-Peer Replication option is not available, am I missing something?

  Answer: Please make sure that you are on Enterprise edition as P2P replication is an Enterprise edition-only feature. And if you are on Enterprise edition, make sure that you have set the **Allow Peer-to-Peer replication** option to **True** in the Transactional Replication's publisher properties under Subscription options.

- **Question**: Could not complete setting up the no-sync subscription at the Distributor while the distribution cleanup agent is running. Does the operation have a greater chance of success if the distribution cleanup agent is temporarily disabled?

  Answer: Stop the Distribution Cleanup Agent and re-create the subscription agent.

- **Question:** There is a conflict detected about duplicate record found for few records on the column that has identity values. How do I rectify it without re-initializing?

  Answer: You may try `-SkipErrors` parameter for the distribution agent or you may delete those rows and re-insert them.

- **Question:** Column name XXX does not exist in the target table or view.

  Answer: Please ensure that the schema are identical, and if they are, make sure that the column that has been reported here is not a calculated column.

Chapter 7: Log Shipping

There are few errors we may encounter with Log Shipping and most of them can be easily resolved. To get them resolved, we can get help from job history. Let's see this with the help of an example.

Frequently asked questions

- **Question 1**: Why do we get the following error?

  Log Shipping is Out of Sync

  We have to dig the SQL Server Error Log and Job History to get more information. Follow these steps to troubleshoot the error:

  1. Expand the **Job Activity Monitor**, right-click on the job, and click **View history**.

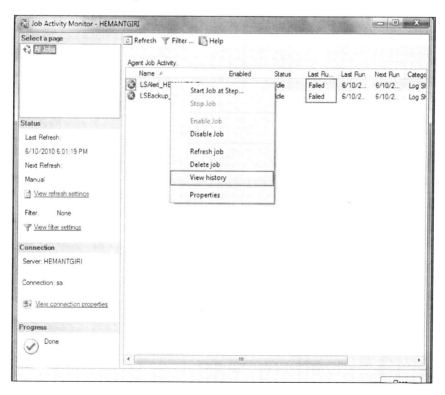

2. As we can see in the error message here, it says that the T-Log restore job has failed to restore the T-Log and is out of sync for the last 59 minutes.

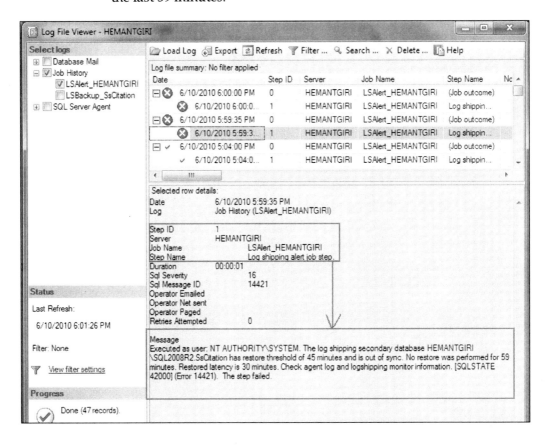

3. We have to carefully see what is causing this job to trigger the error, as this error caused by restoration hasn't occurred for 59 minutes. Let's check the backup job, to see if the backup job was performed successfully before. When checking job history of the backup job, I noticed that the backup job failed because it could not find the network path where we have kept the backup files (see the following screenshot).

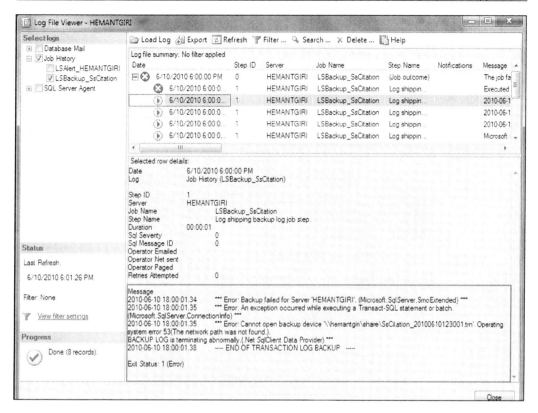

4. The next course of action is to check what has caused the network error. Some of the possible reasons could be:

- Somebody from the system admin team has wiped out the NTFS permission
- The folder that was shared by us is now unshared
- The system has lost the network connection
- Hardware failure (either disk or network)

These are just an example and there could be some other possible reasons too. We have to carefully analyze them to troubleshoot the error.

- **Question 2**: I get the following error:

  The log in this backup set begins at LSN xxxxxxxxxxxxxxx, which is too late to apply to the database. An earlier log backup that includes LSN xxxxxxxxxxxxxxx can be restored.

Or, the following error at times:

Error: The log in this backup set begins at LSN xxxxxxxxxxxxxxx, which is too early to apply to the database. An earlier log backup that includes LSN xxxxxxxxxxxxxxx can be restored.

Answer: The main reason for this error to come up is the T-Log getting truncated. There are a few steps we need to perform to resolve this error.

1. We have to carefully check the last log backup file that was restored on the Secondary Server.

2. Disable all the Log Shipping jobs.

3. Check if the immediate backup file is there in the backup folder. If it is, restore that last backup file with the "No Recovery" or "Standby" option.

4. Enable all the Log Shipping jobs.

   Even the following error is possible:

   Could not apply log backup file "path\file" to secondary database "db", exclusive access could not be obtained because the database is in use.

   The error is self explanatory. It says that while applying a T-Log backup, the SPID could not obtain the exclusive access, which is required to restore database/log backup.

   Answer: We should check the **disconnect users in the database when restoring backups** option. This will disconnect the users while restoring the backup file.

- **Question 3**: My primary server goes down. How can I make my secondary database as primary?

  Answer: There are a few steps we have to perform manually to make secondary database a primary one.

  1. Check if we can have Tail Log backup of the primary database.

  2. If we are able to take Tail Log backup, apply the tail log backup **with Recovery** option while restoring T-Log backup.

  3. If the primary database doesn't allow us to take backup, execute the following command:

     ```
     restore database <dbname> with recovery
     ```

  4. We also need to ensure that the logins and other metadata are in sync with the secondary database.

Chapter 8: Database Mirroring

- **Question:** How do I make sure which port is associated with Database Mirroring?

  Answer: Execute the following code to get the list of port(s) that are associated with the database mirroring:

  ```
  SELECT type_desc, port FROM sys.tcp_endpoints;
  GO
  ```

- **Question:** How do I ensure that endpoints are started?

  Answer: Execute the following code to confirm whether or not the endpoints are started:

  ```
  SELECT state_desc FROM sys.database_mirroring_endpoints
  ```

- **Question:** I am getting Error: 1418; how do I resolve this error?

  Answer: Error 1418 is related to general network error. We have to make sure that the ports we will be using to establish database mirroring are available; also make sure that the firewall are not blocking them.

- **Question:** Principal and Mirror server are not on the same domain or trusted domain; which service accounts do I use?

  Answer: Use the local accounts on the both Principal and Mirror, which has the identical name and password.

- **Question:** How do I ensure that the service account has the CONNECT permission for the endpoints?

  Answer: Execute the following code to confirm whether the service account has the CONNECT permission. Execute this code into both the server to check and confirm.

  ```
  SELECT 'Metadata Check';
  SELECT EP.name, SP.STATE,
     CONVERT(nvarchar(38), suser_name(SP.grantor_principal_id))
        AS GRANTOR,
     SP.TYPE AS PERMISSION,
     CONVERT(nvarchar(46),suser_name(SP.grantee_principal_id))
        AS GRANTEE
     FROM sys.server_permissions SP, sys.endpoints EP
     WHERE SP.major_id = EP.endpoint_id
     ORDER BY Permission, grantor, grantee;
  GO
  ```

- **Question**: My database mirroring session occasionally shows time-out error.

  Answer: Generally synchronous mode (High Safety) has 10 seconds time out value configured. This value is dependent on the ping request being sent between Principal and Mirror server.

  Sometimes the ping acknowledgement comes late due to various reasons such as network congestion or slow processing, but this delay is considered as time out, and depending on the operating mode, it may failover. Hence, it is always recommended to be cautious while configuring the time out value.

  The typical time out value (10 seconds) is good enough. But if we wish, we can increase this value by executing following command:

```
ALTER DATABASE AdventureWorks SET PARTNER TIMEOUT 15
GO
```

  To get the current time out value, execute the following query:

```
SELECT mirroring_connection_timeout
FROM
sys.database_mirroring
GO
```

B

External References

In this appendix we will see external references specific to each chapter.

Chapter 1: Understanding Windows Domain, Domain Users, and SQL Server Security

- What are the different types of RAID array that can be configured in general:

  `http://en.wikipedia.org/wiki/RAID`

- What are the different types of RAID Array that can be configured in SQL Server:

  `http://msdn.microsoft.com/en-us/library/ms190764.aspx`

- Before Installing SQL Server 2008 failover clustering:

  `http://msdn.microsoft.com/en-us/library/ms189910.aspx`

- Configuring the Quorum in a failover clustering:

  `http://technet.microsoft.com/en-us/library/cc770620%28WS.10%29.aspx`

Chapter 2: Implementing Clustering

- General troubleshooting for SQL server failover cluster:

  `http://msdn.microsoft.com/en-us/library/ms189117(SQL.90).aspx`

- Patching SQL server failover cluster:

  `http://support.microsoft.com/kb/958734`

- Before installing SQL server failover clustering:

  `http://technet.microsoft.com/en-us/library/ms189910.aspx`

- Further reading on installing failover cluster using virtual server:

  `https://blogs.msdn.com/blakhani/archive/2007/12/31/how-to-cre-ate-sql-20005-cluster-on-virtual-server.aspx`

- Further reading on installing failover cluster using Hyper-V:

  `http://blogs.technet.com/kevinholman/archive/2008/10/20/set-ting-up-a-2-node-server-2008-failover-cluster-under-hyperv.aspx`

- Further reading for CPU & I/O Affinity Mask configuration:

  `http://msdn.microsoft.com/en-us/library/ms187104.aspx`

- Un-installing SQL server cluster step-by-step:

  `http://www.sql-server-performance.com/articles/clustering/unin-stall_sqlserver_cluster_p1.aspx`

- Upgrading SQL Server 2008 failover cluster instance:

  `http://msdn.microsoft.com/en-us/library/ms191295.aspx`

- Implication of clustering on replication:

  `http://www.sql-server-performance.com/faq/clustering_replica-tion_p1.aspx`

- Paul Randel's blog on adding GEO redundancy to failover clustering:

  `http://www.sqlskills.com/BLOGS/PAUL/post/Adding-geo-redundancy-to-failover-clustering.aspx`

- High Availability: Interoperability and Co-existence:

  `http://msdn.microsoft.com/en-us/library/bb500117.aspx` and

  `http://social.msdn.microsoft.com/Forums/en/sqlreplication/thread/842774e4-dbc0-4df4-8022-c1ce20f369b7`

- Deploying cluster shared volumes in Windows Server 2008 R2 failover clustering:

  `http://blogs.msdn.com/b/clustering/archive/2009/02/19/9433146.aspx`

- Top 10 Articles for SQL server clustering:

  `http://www.sql-server-citation.com/2010/02/top-10-articles-on-sql-server.html`

Chapter 3: Snapshot Replication

- For detailed information on the different parameters for Snapshot Agent:

  `http://msdn.microsoft.com/en-us/library/ms146939.aspx`

- For detailed information on the different parameters for Distribution Agent:

  `http://msdn.microsoft.com/en-us/library/ms147328.aspx`

- Subscription expiration and retention period

  `http://msdn.microsoft.com/en-us/library/ms151188.aspx`

- Performance tuning tips for Snapshot Replication by Brad McGehee, SQL Server MVP:

  `http://www.sql-server-performance.com/tips/snapshot_replica-tion_tuning_p1.aspx`

- Deprecated features of replication:

  `http://Technet.microsoft.com/en-us/library/ms143550.aspx`

- How to resolve invalidate snapshot error:

  `http://social.msdn.microsoft.com/forums/en-US/sqlreplication/thread/f01a1fef-dcf8-4673-a172-4063888a046c/`

- List of error codes and its description:

  `http://msdn.microsoft.com/en-us/library/aa937600%28SQL.80%29.aspx`

- How to add an article to Snapshot Replication:

  `http://msdn.microsoft.com/en-us/library/ms146887.aspx`

- What is new in the Replication Monitor in SQL Server 2008 – Paul Ibison:

  `http://replicationanswers.com/SQL2008GUI.asp`

- General FAQ for SQL Server Replication – Paul Ibison:

  `http://replicationanswers.com/General.asp`

- Enhancing Snapshot Replication performance:

  `http://msdn.microsoft.com/en-us/library/aa237430%28v=SQL.80%29.aspx`

- Configure non-SQL server subscriber:

  `http://technet.microsoft.com/en-us/library/ms151195.aspx`

- Configure non-SQL server publication:

  `http://msdn.microsoft.com/en-us/library/ms151243.aspx`

- Replication over Internet

  `http://msdn.microsoft.com/en-us/library/ms151319.aspx`

- Securing replication over Internet:

  `http://msdn.microsoft.com/en-us/library/ms151172.aspx`

- Replication monitor performance:

  `http://msdn.microsoft.com/en-us/library/ms152482.aspx`

Chapter 4: Transactional Replication

- Selecting an account for SQL Server Agent service:

  `http://msdn.microsoft.com/en-us/library/ms191543.aspx`

- Supported service account type for SQL Server Agent

  `http://msdn.microsoft.com/en-us/library/ms345380.aspx`

- Skipping errors in Transactional Replication

  `http://msdn.microsoft.com/en-us/library/ms151331(v=SQL.105).aspx`

- Controlling constraints, identities and triggers with Not for Replication

  `http://msdn.microsoft.com/en-us/library/ms152529(v=SQL.105).aspx`

- Updatable subscription for Transaction Replication

  `http://msdn.microsoft.com/en-us/library/ms151718(v=SQL.105).aspx`

- Changes in SQL Server Replication SQL 2008

  `http://msdn.microsoft.com/en-us/library/ms143470.aspx`

- What is new in replication?

  `http://msdn.microsoft.com/en-us/library/bb500342(v=SQL.105).aspx`

- Performance tuning and optimization with Transactional Replication

  `http://technet.microsoft.com/en-us/library/cc966539.aspx`

- How to specify schema options

  `http://msdn.microsoft.com/en-us/library/ms147887(v=SQL.105).aspx`

- How to massively optimize transactional replication – Paul Ibison

  `http://replicationanswers.com/TransactionalOptimisation.asp`

- Handling Identity columns in P2P transactional replication on SQL Server 2005/2008 – Paul Ibison

  `http://replicationanswers.com/P2PIdentities.asp`

- Subscription deactivation and expiration

  `http://msdn.microsoft.com/en-us/library/Aa178794`

- How to enable replication agent for logging to output files

  `http://support.microsoft.com/kb/312292`

- Managing identity values in replication

  `http://www.simple-talk.com/sql/database-administration/the-identity-crisis-in-replication/`

Chapter 5: Merge Replication

- Good article on conflict resolution:

  `http://msdn.microsoft.com/en-us/library/ms151749.aspx`

- How web synchronization works:

  `http://msdn.microsoft.com/en-us/library/ms151763.aspx`

- Strategies for backing up and restoring Merge Replication:

  `http://msdn.microsoft.com/en-us/library/ms152497.aspx`

- Backing up and restoring replicated databases:

  `http://msdn.microsoft.com/en-us/library/ms151152.aspx`

- Best practice for Replication Administration:

  `http://msdn.microsoft.com/en-us/library/ms151818.aspx`

- Merge Replication basic troubleshooting

  `http://support.microsoft.com/kb/315521`

- How Merge Replication tracks changes

  `http://msdn.microsoft.com/en-us/library/ms151789.aspx`

- Advance Merge Replication conflict detection and resolution

  `http://msdn.microsoft.com/en-us/library/ms151257.aspx`

- Getting error codes and description information

  `http://msdn.microsoft.com/en-us/library/ms182485.aspx`

- Sys views for replication

  `http://msdn.microsoft.com/en-us/library/ms187369.aspx`

- System tables for replication

  `http://msdn.microsoft.com/en-us/library/ms179855.aspx`

- Common issues in the Merge Replication

  `http://www.replicationanswers.com/Merge.asp`

- Parameterised row filters

  http://msdn.microsoft.com/en-us/library/ms152478.aspx

Chapter 6: Peer-to-Peer Replication

- How to view conflicts:

  http://technet.microsoft.com/en-us/library/ms151865.aspx

- Transactional Replication FAQ – Paul Ibison:

  http://www.replicationanswers.com/Transactional.asp

- Strategies for backing up and restoring snapshot and Transactional Replication:

  http://msdn.microsoft.com/en-us/library/ms152560.aspx

- New replication features in SQL Server 2008:

  http://searchsqlserver.techtarget.com/tip/New-replication-features-in-SQL-Server-2008-and-what-they-mean-to-you

- New replication features in SQL Server 2008 – Kasim Wirama:

  http://netindonesia.net/blogs/kasim.wirama/archive/2008/06/15/peer-to-peer-replication-in-sql-server-2008.aspx

- Replication security best practices:

  http://msdn.microsoft.com/en-us/library/ms151227.aspx

- How to administer a Peer-to-Peer topology:

  http://msdn.microsoft.com/en-us/library/ms146867.aspx

- Replicating identity columns:

  http://technet.microsoft.com/en-us/library/ms152543.aspx

- How to start and stop replication agent:

  http://technet.microsoft.com/en-us/library/ms151783.aspx

Chapter 7: Log Shipping

- Backup compression:

  http://technet.microsoft.com/en-us/library/bb964719.aspx

- Optimizing backup and restore performance in SQL server

  http://msdn.microsoft.com/en-us/library/ms190954.aspx

- White Paper: Data Compression – Strategy, Capacity Planning and Best Practices:

  `http://msdn.microsoft.com/en-us/library/dd894051.aspx`

- Data compression in SQL Server 2008:

  `http://www.sql-server-performance.com/articles/dba/Data_Com-pression_in_SQL_Server_2008_p1.aspx`

- Types of data compression in SQL server 2008:

  `http://blogs.msdn.com/b/sqlserverstorageengine/ar-chive/2007/11/12/types-of-data-compression-in-sql-server-2008.aspx`

- Restoring a log shipping log backup be slow:

  `http://sqlskills.com/BLOGS/PAUL/post/Why-could-restoring-a-log-shipping-log-backup-be-slow.aspx`

- Description of the effects of non-logged and minimally logged operations on transaction log backup and the restore process in SQL Server:

  `http://support.microsoft.com/kb/272093`

- BUG: There is a chance to get the following message while performing role switching: **sp_change_secondary_role Fails with Error 3101**. Here is the work around to follow:

  `http://support.microsoft.com/kb/294397`

- Managing metadata when making a database available on another server:

  `http://msdn.microsoft.com/en-us/library/ms187580.aspx`

- What is Tail Log backup and when it is useful:

  `http://msdn.microsoft.com/en-us/library/ms179314.aspx`

- How to get the sp_help_revlogin:

  `http://support.microsoft.com/kb/918992/en-us`

- How to resolve permission issues when you move a database between servers that are running SQL server:

  `http://support.microsoft.com/kb/240872`

- Sync all logins on a server in a single click using sp_msforeachdb:

  `http://www.sqlservercentral.com/articles/Log+Shipping/63028/`

Chapter 8: Database Mirroring

- Managing metadata when making a database available on another server instance:

  http://msdn.microsoft.com/en-us/library/ms187580.aspx

- Using certificates for Database Mirroring:

  http://msdn.microsoft.com/en-us/library/ms191477.aspx

- Monitoring mirroring status:

  http://msdn.microsoft.com/en-us/library/ms365781.aspx

- Using warning thresholds and alerts on mirror performance metrics:

  http://msdn.microsoft.com/en-us/library/ms408393.aspx

- Database Mirroring metadata:

  http://msdn.microsoft.com/en-us/library/ms366276.aspx

- How to view the status of the mirrored database using Management Studio:

  http://msdn.microsoft.com/en-us/library/ms187050.aspx

- Estimating the interruption of service during role switching:

  http://msdn.microsoft.com/en-us/library/ms187465.aspx

- Configuring replication with Database Mirroring:

  http://msdn.microsoft.com/en-us/library/ms151799.aspx

Index

Symbols

A

B

C

U

Utility Control Point (UCP) 34

V

Virtual PC (VPC) 34

W

web synchronization
  URL 277
windows authentication mode
  Application Role 12
  Fixed DB Role 11

Fixed Server Roles 10, 11
  Mixed Authentication 12
windows domain 8
witness server, database mirroring
  adding 242-245
witness server, database mirroring
  component 224

X

XY Incorporation 137

Thank you for buying

Microsoft SQL Server 2008 High Availability

About Packt Publishing

Packt, pronounced 'packed', published its first book "Mastering phpMyAdmin for Effective MySQL Management" in April 2004 and subsequently continued to specialize in publishing highly focused books on specific technologies and solutions.

Our books and publications share the experiences of your fellow IT professionals in adapting and customizing today's systems, applications, and frameworks. Our solution based books give you the knowledge and power to customize the software and technologies you're using to get the job done. Packt books are more specific and less general than the IT books you have seen in the past. Our unique business model allows us to bring you more focused information, giving you more of what you need to know, and less of what you don't.

Packt is a modern, yet unique publishing company, which focuses on producing quality, cutting-edge books for communities of developers, administrators, and newbies alike. For more information, please visit our website: www.packtpub.com.

About Packt Enterprise

In 2010, Packt launched two new brands, Packt Enterprise and Packt Open Source, in order to continue its focus on specialization. This book is part of the Packt Enterprise brand, home to books published on enterprise software – software created by major vendors, including (but not limited to) IBM, Microsoft and Oracle, often for use in other corporations. Its titles will offer information relevant to a range of users of this software, including administrators, developers, architects, and end users.

Writing for Packt

We welcome all inquiries from people who are interested in authoring. Book proposals should be sent to author@packtpub.com. If your book idea is still at an early stage and you would like to discuss it first before writing a formal book proposal, contact us; one of our commissioning editors will get in touch with you.

We're not just looking for published authors; if you have strong technical skills but no writing experience, our experienced editors can help you develop a writing career, or simply get some additional reward for your expertise.

Learning SQL Server 2008 Reporting Services

ISBN: 978-1-847196-18-7   Paperback: 512 pages

A step-by-step guide to getting the most of Microsoft SQL Server Reporting Services 2008

1. Everything you need to create and deliver data-rich reports with SQL Server 2008 Reporting Services as quickly as possible

2. Packed with hands-on-examples to learn and improve your skills

3. Connect and report from databases, spreadsheets, XML Data, and more

4. No experience of SQL Server Reporting Services required

Expert Cube Development with Microsoft SQL Server 2008 Analysis Services

ISBN: 978-1-847197-22-1   Paperback: 360 pages

Design and implement fast, scalable and maintainable cubes

1. A real-world guide to designing cubes with Analysis Services 2008

2. Model dimensions and measure groups in BI Development Studio

3. Implement security, drill-through, and MDX calculations

4. Learn how to deploy, monitor, and performance-tune your cube

5. Filled with best practices and useful hints and tips

Please check **www.PacktPub.com** for information on our titles

LaVergne, TN USA
25 January 2011
213914LV00003B/52/P

9 781849 681223